Bob Weih

Enterprise GIS for Energy Companies

Christian Harder

ESRI Press

Published by
Environmental Systems Research Institute, Inc.
380 New York Street
Redlands, California 92373-8100

Environmental Systems Research Institute, Inc.
Enterprise GIS for Energy Companies
ISBN 1-879102-48-X

Contents

Preface

Practically everything an electric or gas utility does has something to do with geography: maintaining pipelines and transmission lines, building and operating power stations, making service calls, responding to emergencies. Everything takes place within the context of, and is thus manageable according to, location. So it is not surprising that utilities all over the world use geographic information systems (GIS) to manage their operations. If you want to keep track of how often a certain type of valve needs replacing, or which service crew to send where, GIS is an obvious solution.

Less obvious is an engineer's need for land ownership data, or that of an operations manager for customer demographics. When all of a company's data is managed from a common spatially referenced database, and information is generally accessible, everyone better understands not only their own work, but how their efforts mesh with those of the larger organization.

Engineers who would ordinarily only deal with CAD data can now see, thanks to GIS, how their work relates to environmental issues, to marketing concerns, to land ownership. Repair crews en route to remote sites, who in the past had no way of knowing what they were driving over or (in extreme cases) bulldozing through, are now given GIS-generated information about access routes and areas to avoid, along with details about their destination and what needs to be repaired there. GIS gives planners of a new pipeline or power station a wide-angle view of the system their project plugs into.

GIS rewires organizations, integrating units that formerly were able to access only the particular information they were thought to need. Indeed, with GIS as a framework, companies discover a whole new vision of what "need" means.

Jack Dangermond
President, ESRI

Acknowledgments

As with all of the books in this ESRI Press series, this one could not have been created without the cooperation of the dozen companies from around the world who allowed us to document the interesting and important work that they do. They supplied the necessary screen shots and background information, and generously gave of their time to review the chapters once completed. You'll find the individuals from these organizations acknowledged at the end of each case study.

Several people from Miner and Miner Consulting Engineers, Inc., also lent their expertise to help make sure the book accurately represented the work they have done in helping many of the featured utilities get their leading-edge geographic information systems up and running. Thanks are due Miner and Miner staff members Bob Lyhus, Jeff Meyers, Brad Shannon, and Susan Powell.

A number of people at ESRI also contributed time and effort. Linda Hecht initiated the development and identified potential case study organizations (some of which have been champions of ESRI products since long before GIS was as popular as it is today). Jesse Theodore, Julio Olimpio, Lee Ross, and Angus Wood also helped pull together some of the stories.

Michael Karman and Tim Ormsby edited the manuscript with their usual attention to detail and readability. Michael Hyatt designed the book, laid out and produced the pages, and handled copyediting and proofreading chores. Judy Boyd and Bill Miller didn't try (too hard) to talk me out of it when I volunteered to write this book.

And finally, the original ESRI employee, Jack Dangermond, committed the resources for yet another ESRI Press title because he believes so strongly in the power of GIS to make just about any type of organization work better.

Chapter 1

The business of energy

In the 1980s, deregulation pushed the telecommunications industry into the competitive world of the marketplace. The same deregulatory forces are now hastening electric and gas utilities into the same world, a world in which the competitive edge comes from the latest technology. Increasingly, utilities are finding geographic information systems (GIS) indispensable, for everything from automated mapping and facilities management to customer service and technician dispatch and routing. And in the process of integrating all of these tasks with a common database across the network, utilities are discovering that their overall operations are more coordinated and efficient.

The spatial revolution in utilities

On a sweltering summer day, in a room filled with computers and wall screens, utility personnel track power consumption in their city. Elsewhere in the room, as temperatures soar outside, brokers hoping to get through the day without a blackout negotiate with other utilities to buy power.

Two floors below, looking at digital maps showing where all the power customers are, customer service reps take calls. From their workstations, they can access all the data they need to answer any question.

Across the hall, an engineer puts the finishing touches on plans to hook up a new subdivision to the power grid.

At the yard, service crews carrying laptop computers loaded with interactive route maps are dispatched throughout the city.

While each of these departments has very different responsibilities, they all use a common spatial database—a GIS—to do their work.

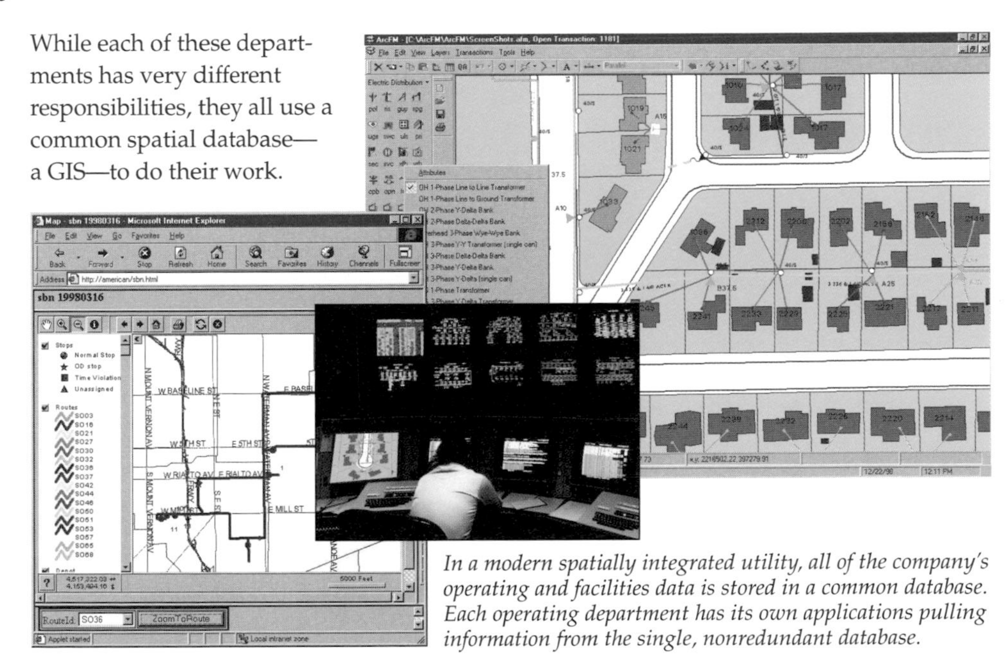

In a modern spatially integrated utility, all of the company's operating and facilities data is stored in a common database. Each operating department has its own applications pulling information from the single, nonredundant database.

The utility information model

Electricity and natural gas are distributed to consumers through some of the most extensive and complicated networks ever engineered. These networks are made up of myriad wires and pipes, transformers and valves, meters and poles.

What a utility must do is make sure that all parts of the system are operational at all times, and it must regulate consumers' connections and disconnections from the system. This is a huge job. But it is made substantially easier when every component of the system (every line, pole, meter) is tracked in a database and easier still when this database is spatial (i.e., a geographic information system, or GIS). In a GIS, the actual physical structure of the distribution system—where the lines run, where the connections are—can be duplicated or modeled on the computer, as can all of the other things, like streets, buildings, and land ownership boundaries, that have a bearing on the distribution system.

The utility information model slices reality into layers. Each layer graphically represents a certain type of feature—roads, power poles, gas meters, transmission lines, and so forth. Every feature is stored in a common database and includes coordinates that allow the computer to draw the feature in its correct place.

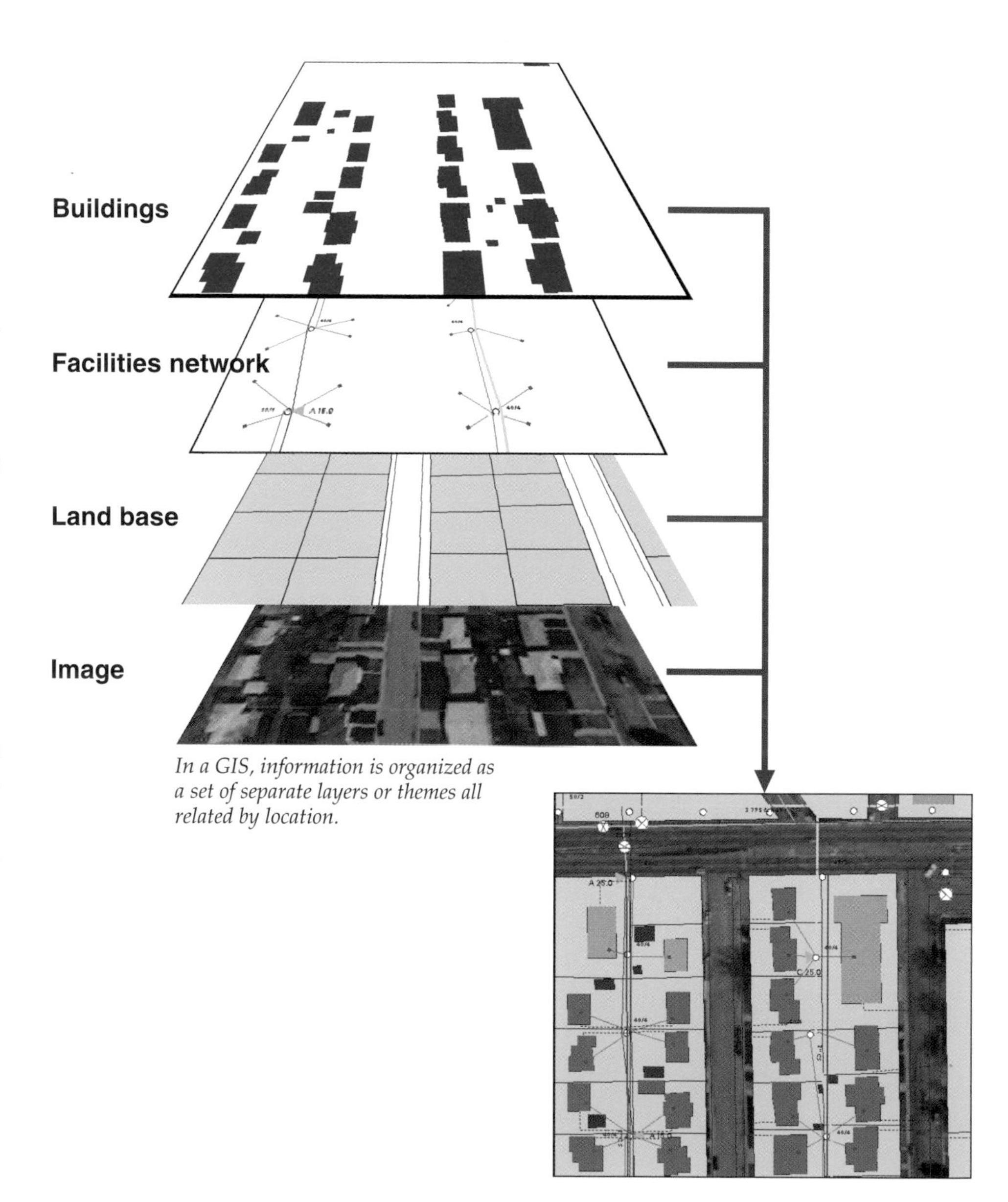

In a GIS, information is organized as a set of separate layers or themes all related by location.

The evolution of enterprise GIS

In the early days of GIS in utilities, each department (real estate, operations, engineering) would build GIS applications to solve its own problems. As these standalone systems evolved, and word of their success spread through the organization, other departments would make connections to the database and build their own applications.

As the use of GIS spread from the engineering department to the dispatcher's office to the call center, and these various departments began sharing information, management often discovered that integrating operations across a common spatial database could result in serendipitous benefits. Engineers could consider environmental data; marketers could study customer complaints; operations managers could comment on design plans before things got built.

Today, many utilities are realizing the benefits of designing their GIS to be "enterprisewide" from the ground up. On the assumption that all departments can benefit from GIS, technology managers at utilities around the globe are building geographic information systems to organize and manage all of their activities with a common spatial database.

GIS at work

There are hundreds of ways in which utilities around the world have made use of GIS, but, broadly speaking, most of the applications fall into one of five areas: operations, engineering, marketing, financial, and mapping.

Operations

The everyday task of the utility is to manage facilities and monitor their use. Facilities are the collection of wires, pipes, poles, transformers, meters, valves, and other hardware for distributing a utility's product. The mapping of these assets on digital maps was the original application of GIS in the utility sector, and is referred to as AM/FM, for automated mapping/facilities management.

Outage management systems allow utilities to respond quickly when weather or equipment failures result in loss of service to any customer. In addition to helping managers determine exactly what caused an outage and what needs to happen to correct it, the latest GIS-based outage management systems are also used to dispatch service crews and to monitor the status of repair activities in the field.

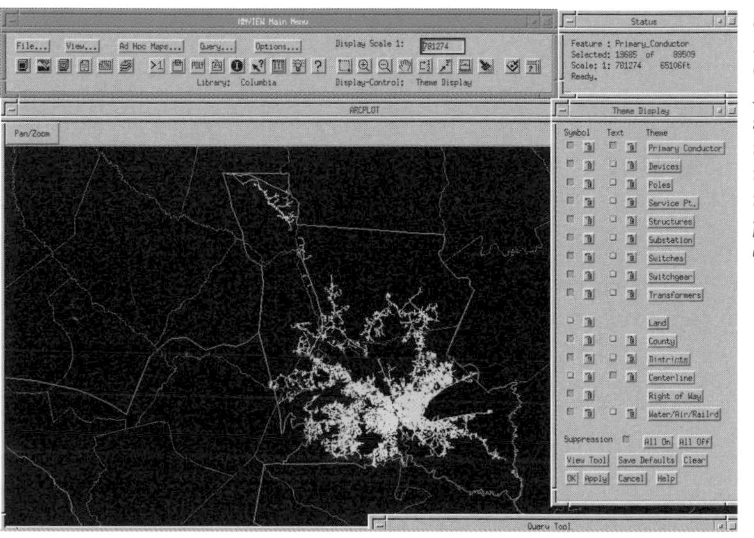

South Carolina Electric & Gas Company uses ARC/INFO® software to manage its distribution network. In the map seen here, primary conductors are shown.

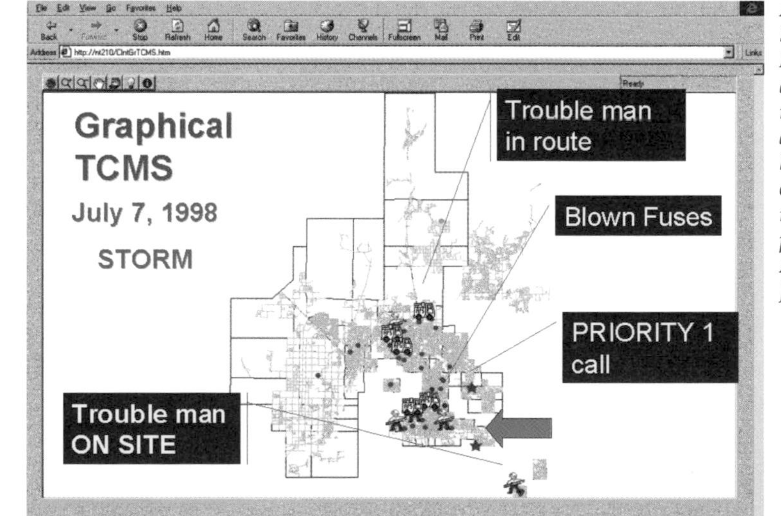

Arizona Public Service's Trouble Call Management System displays call information by severity, and also shows the location and status of repair crews. This map shows metropolitan Phoenix, Arizona, during a July 1998 storm.

Utilities spend significant time and money on logistics—the deployment of people and equipment. Logistics problems lend themselves naturally to a GIS solution. Because logistics involves the analysis of a network different than utilities historically work with (streets instead of power lines and pipelines), many utilities have been slow to realize the potential benefit of applying GIS. But with powerful and easy-to-use software like ArcLogistics™ Route now available, many utilities are finding they can save millions of dollars annually preplanning the driving routes followed by their sizable fleets of vehicles.

GIS also helps utilities forecast and schedule the material, labor, and equipment resources needed for any given project. This is known in the business as work management.

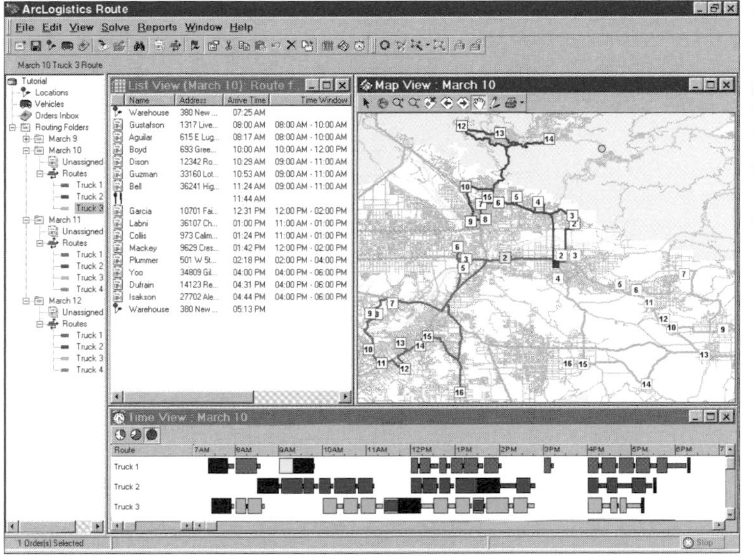

Southern California Gas Company uses GIS-based routing software to determine which vehicles should respond to service calls and what the best route to get there should be.

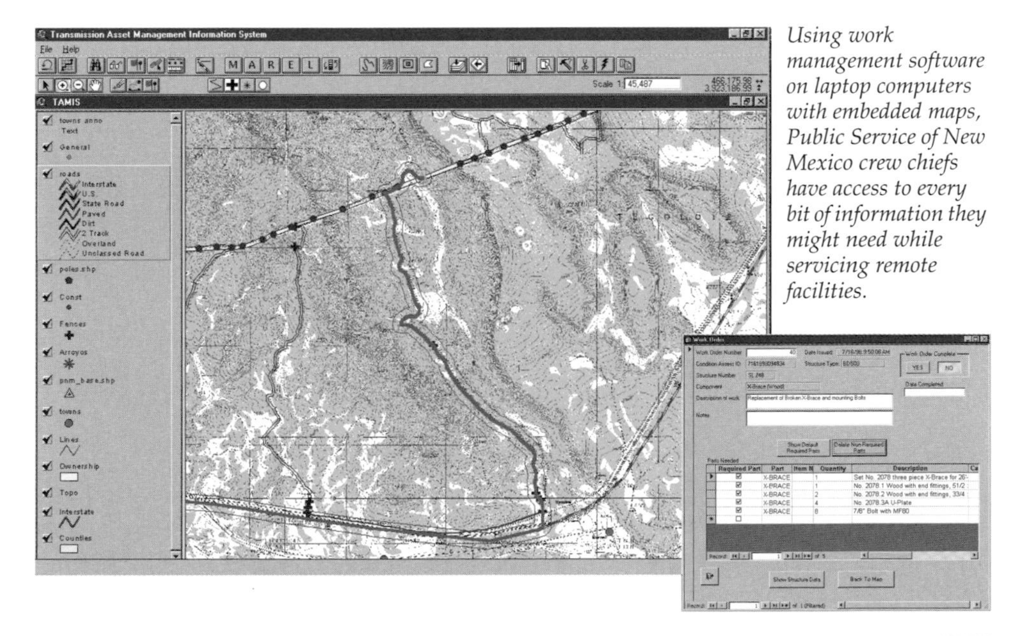

Using work management software on laptop computers with embedded maps, Public Service of New Mexico crew chiefs have access to every bit of information they might need while servicing remote facilities.

As they begin operating more like competitive companies and less like monopolies, energy providers are putting new emphasis on providing quality customer service. Information technology has raised consumer expectations, and utilities are learning important service lessons from private companies. One of these lessons is that GIS can be used to give quick answers to customer inquiries. During a power outage, for example, support representatives can check digital maps on their desktops and inform callers about the precise extent of the outage and, more importantly, the expected time until power will be restored.

Perhaps no aspect of the energy company's purview is more important than its ability to respond to a natural disaster or other emergency that causes widespread damage to facilities. Lives are at stake when the power goes out in a northeastern ice storm or a heat wave in Chicago. By using GIS to distribute crucial information to emergency response teams, modern utilities have kept many life-threatening situations under control.

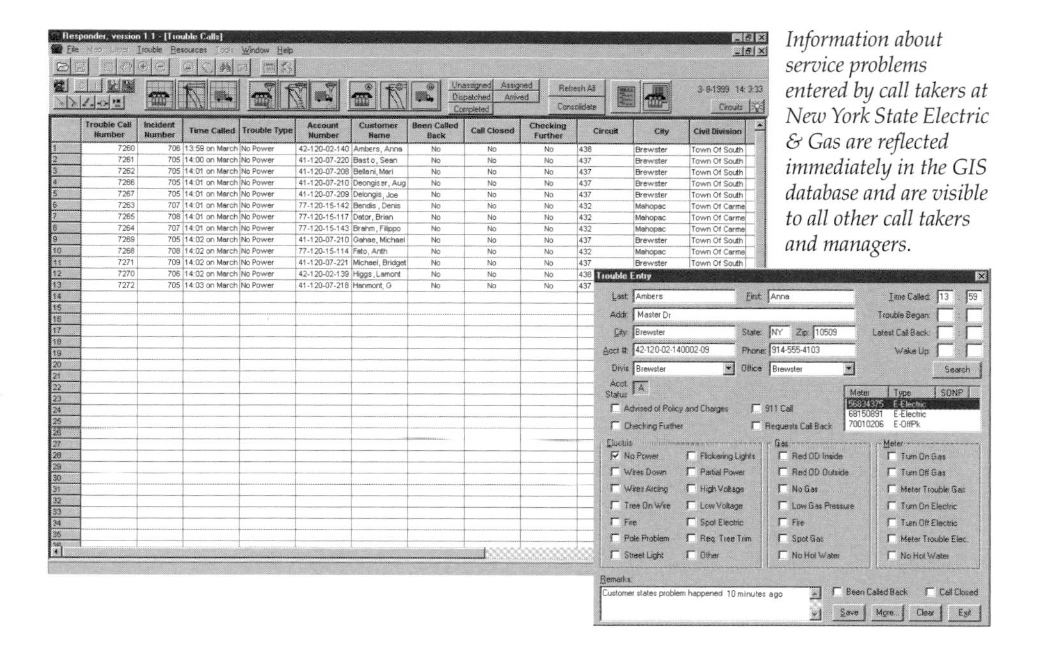

Information about service problems entered by call takers at New York State Electric & Gas are reflected immediately in the GIS database and are visible to all other call takers and managers.

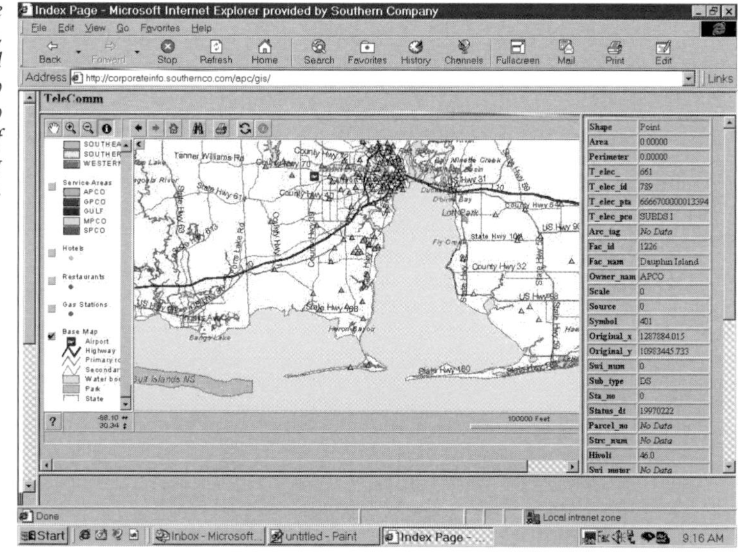

During Hurricane Georges in 1998, Alabama Power used the World Wide Web to disseminate maps to the hundreds of employees converging on Mobile.

Engineering

The engineering department of a power utility designs and coordinates the construction of new facilities and the upgrade of existing equipment. In areas experiencing rapid housing development, the design of utility infrastructure can often become a bottleneck in the building process. Automating the design process means using GIS software and database information to reduce construction costs and speed up the development process.

Using GIS and real-time data from the distribution system, engineers can also analyze the performance of the gas or electrical network without ever leaving their computer terminals. The entire system can be modeled to evaluate its performance in terms of reliability, power loss, capacity, or any number of other criteria. In Beirut, Lebanon, the network is routinely analyzed to ferret out illegal connections made to the system.

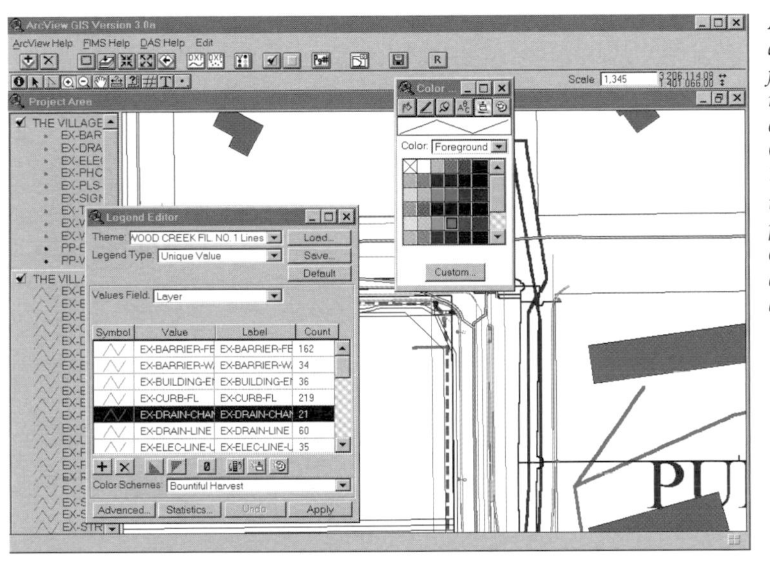

Automating the design of new facilities to serve residential construction allows Colorado Springs Utilities to streamline the development process and save tens of thousands of dollars on each new design.

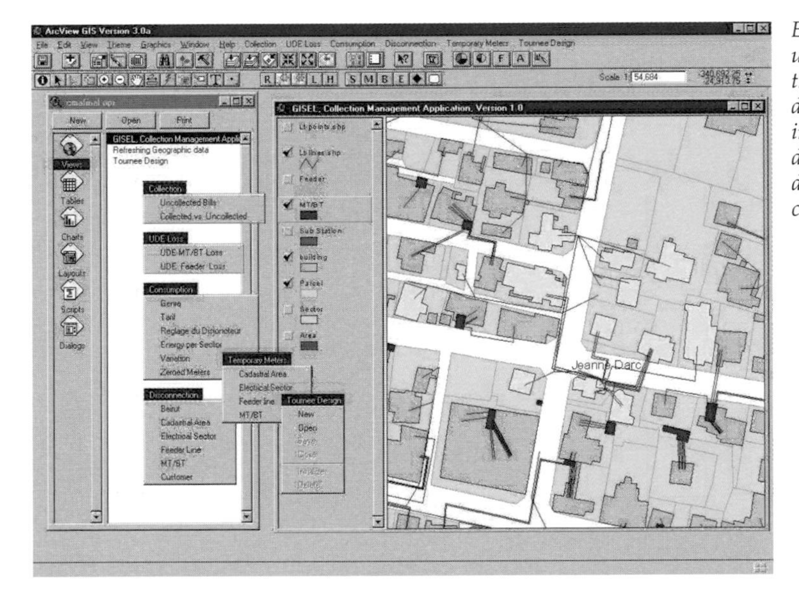

Electricité du Liban uses GIS to analyze the performance of its distribution system in Beirut, a system damaged heavily during Lebanon's civil war.

Marketing

Deregulation of the energy business has created a new focus on marketing and customer research. Consumers in many parts of the United States now choose their energy providers, so utilities are building new products and services and expanding into new markets. As their counterparts in the business world learned many years ago, GIS is an ideal tool for conducting demographic research.

As part of this new marketing emphasis, utilities are also working hard to improve the level of customer service they deliver. As entities that exist in space, utilities are finding that maps are a user-friendly way to convey all sorts of information to customers, both in printed form and as electronic documents delivered on the Internet.

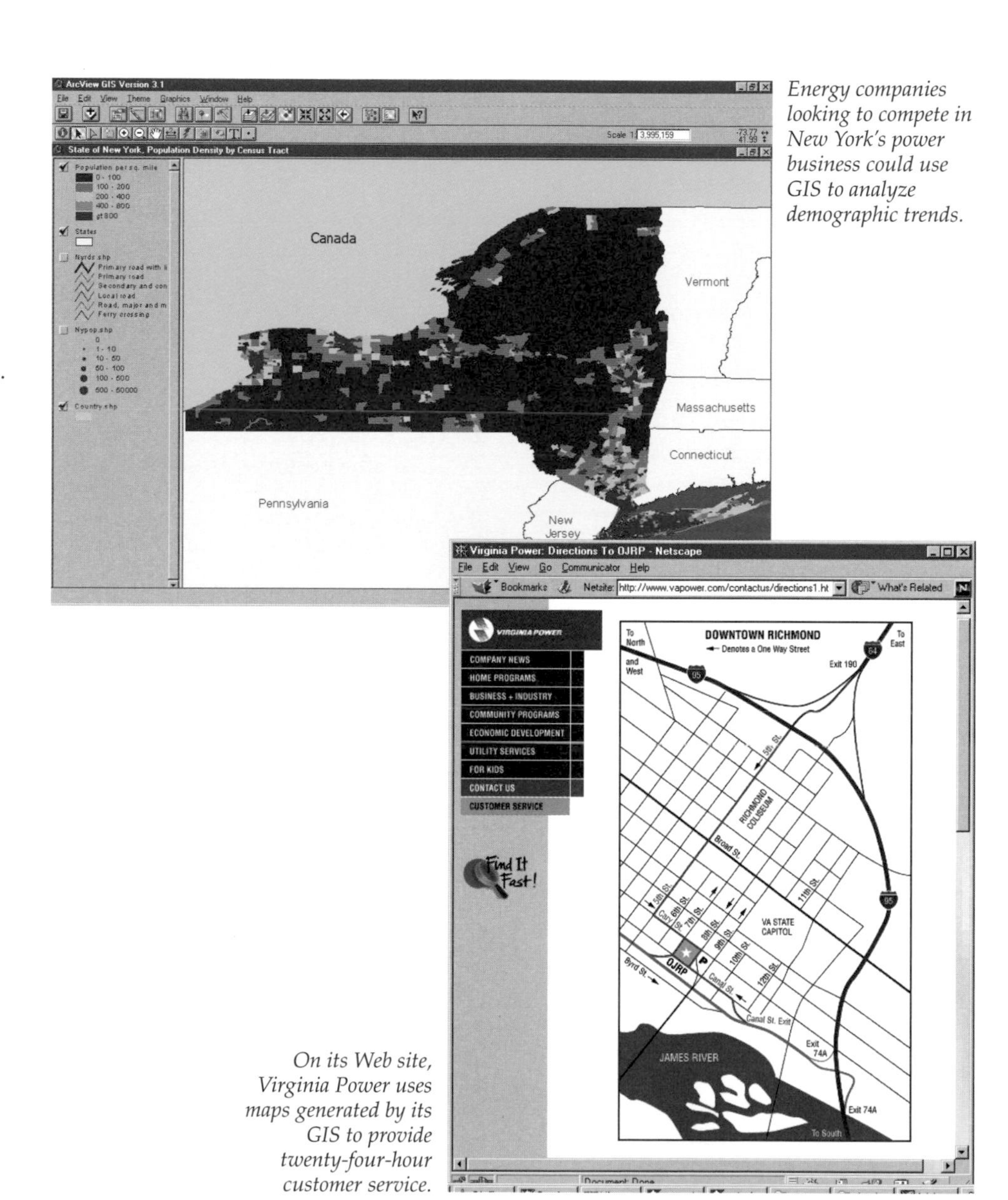

Energy companies looking to compete in New York's power business could use GIS to analyze demographic trends.

On its Web site, Virginia Power uses maps generated by its GIS to provide twenty-four-hour customer service.

Finance and compliance

There's really no job at a utility that can't be made easier with geographic information. Finance departments are responsible for, among other things, asset purchasing and accounting systems. Whereas traditional databases store asset information entirely in tables, a spatially integrated database provides a map-based view of assets that a financial manager may never see in person.

Although they are being gradually deregulated in terms of how they compete in the marketplace, utilities are still required to adhere to local laws. This involves not only compliance, but also documenting that compliance. GIS gives utilities a powerful tool for implementing practices that adhere to regulations, and for communicating their compliance to a diverse audience of shareholders, legislators, regulatory officials, and the general public.

A GIS database allows an asset manager to view, sort, and analyze, in a map-based view, information about all of a company's equipment. The information shown here is for a secondary conductor in Greely, Colorado.

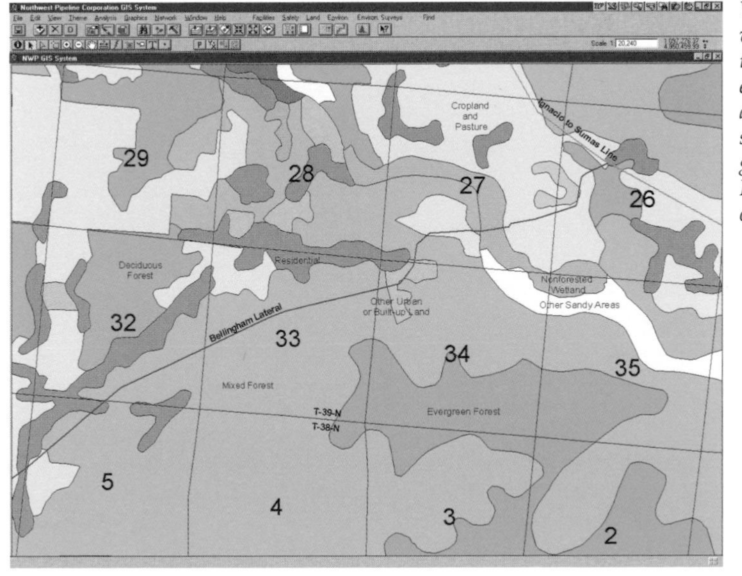

Williams Gas Pipeline, which operates safely through many ecologically sensitive areas, complies with strict environmental guidelines in the Pacific Northwest with the help of its GIS.

Tales from the real world

The next twelve chapters take you behind the scenes at a dozen utilities from around the world.

You'll learn of the specific applications that these companies have developed in support of their own local operations, and you'll also begin to gain a sense of how they have all integrated their various departments through a common paradigm: that of geography. By working on a common spatial database, these organizations are coordinating work among departments, and operating more effectively.

After reading the case studies, you can begin to explore the technology itself by studying the appendix about ArcFM™ software, an off-the-shelf ARC/INFO application developed by Environmental Systems Research Institute (ESRI), Inc., and Miner and Miner.

Chapter 2

When the power fails

When the electricity goes out, that's inconvenient. When it goes out during a winter storm, that could be dangerous or even fatal. Since many outages happen during inclement weather as a result of lightning strikes or ice buildup on power lines, utility managers must be ready to identify the cause of the failure and get the power back on as quickly as possible.

In this chapter, you'll see how New York State Electric & Gas Corporation, with consulting engineers Miner and Miner, developed a system that speeds up response time from hours to minutes. The solution is an integrated client/server application called "Responder."

Powering a cold-weather state

New York State Electric & Gas Corporation, albeit a 145-year-old business concern, is a prime example of a modern, market-driven energy company. With a service area that covers more than half the state (excluding New York City), NYSEG distributes electricity to over 800,000 customers and natural gas to nearly a quarter million homes. The company also sells power in northeast and mid-Atlantic wholesale electricity markets.

Located as it is in a part of the country notorious for its severe winter weather, NYSEG is no stranger to frequent and extensive outages. Recently, it updated the technology used to manage these situations.

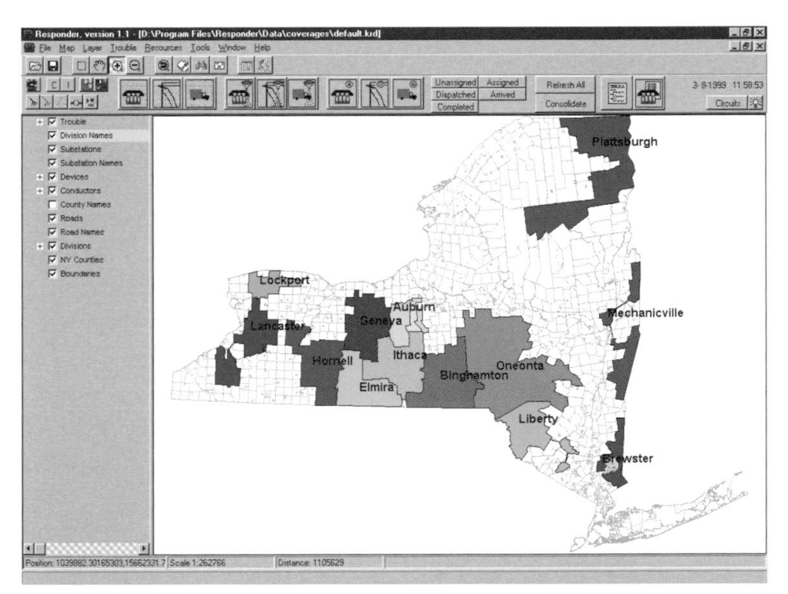

NYSEG uses a trouble call management system called Responder to deal with outage response.

No power

Lightning storms are among the most common causes of weather-related power outages. The following pages describe how Responder might be used in a situation where widespread lightning has knocked out power at various locations across the NYSEG service territory.

Telephone agents working in NYSEG's call centers keep a Trouble Entry form open on their computer screens for entering callers' addresses and for checking off their problems on a list. During a lightning storm, the majority of calls reported "no power."

Once all the details are captured, the agent can bring up a screen that shows other customers in the same neighborhood and whether or not they too have called NYSEG. If there is a known problem in the area (as there is in the screen shown below right), the agent will see that and be able to tell the caller that the incident has been noticed and that help is on the way.

Even before the caller has hung up the line, the new information has been automatically passed on to Responder and the analysis process begins.

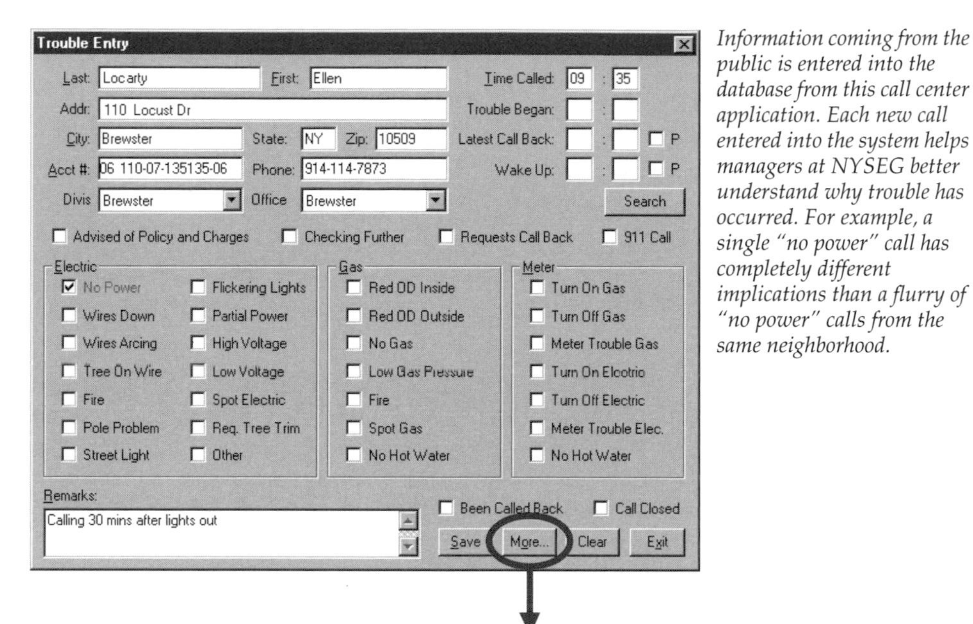

Information coming from the public is entered into the database from this call center application. Each new call entered into the system helps managers at NYSEG better understand why trouble has occurred. For example, a single "no power" call has completely different implications than a flurry of "no power" calls from the same neighborhood.

Additional Information

This customer is most likely involved with an outage at substation TILLY FOSTER, circuit 437, line 1620, and pole 13.

Customer First Called: 09:34 AM on October 20, 1998
Times: 1
First Call Taken By: Control Energy
Affected: 47

Customer on same transfomer as the caller.

Name	Address	City	Called
Belli, Michael	Locust Dr	Brewster	No
Barglecki, Janet	Locust Dr	Brewster	Yes
Boms, Rosaria A.	Brewster Hill Rd	Brewster	No
Hordie, Richard	Locust Dr	Brewster	No
Roms, Katheeen M	Locust Dr	Brewster	No
Sotiro, Mich	Locust Dr	Brewster	No
Raylor, Richard	Locust Dr	Brewster	No

Outage Begin Time: 04:35 PM on October 19, 1998
Status: Unassigned
Time:
Estimated Restortion Time:
Cause of Outage:
Field Comment:
Return

Trouble Call Analysis engine

As calls are entered into the system, a Responder component known as the Trouble Call Analysis (TCA) engine runs in the background, grouping calls by transformer and finding the devices that qualify as the most probable cause of the outage. The most probable outage devices are analyzed and classified as incidents. The incidents are grouped and prioritized so they can be dispatched to repair crews.

In the screen at the right, green circles have been drawn over two fuses that the TCA engine has determined to be the most likely suspects. The circuitry connected to these fuses has been shaded black to indicate that it is de-energized. The records highlighted in yellow are the incidents created by Responder that need to be dealt with by the dispatcher's office.

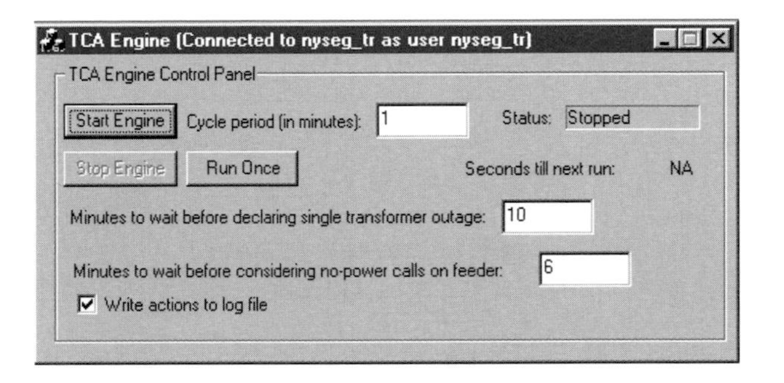

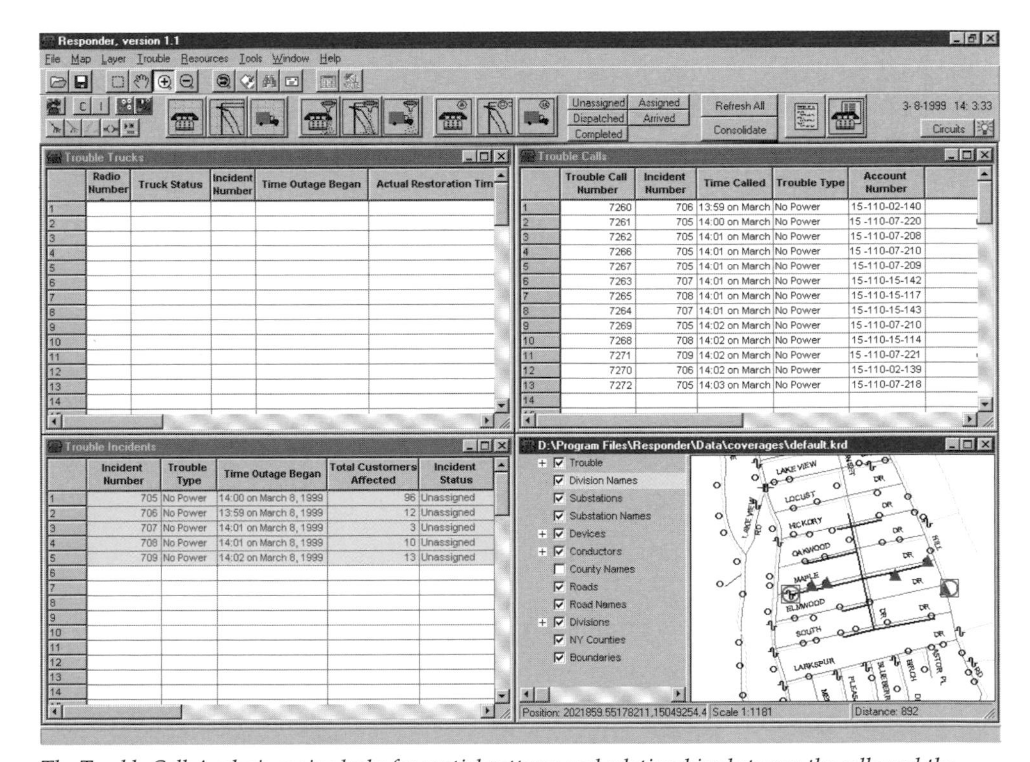

	Trouble Call Number	Incident Number	Time Called	Trouble Type	Account Number
1	7260	706	13:59 on March	No Power	15-110-02-140
2	7261	705	14:00 on March	No Power	15-110-07-220
3	7262	705	14:01 on March	No Power	15-110-07-208
4	7266	705	14:01 on March	No Power	15-110-07-210
5	7267	705	14:01 on March	No Power	15-110-07-209
6	7263	707	14:01 on March	No Power	15-110-15-142
7	7265	708	14:01 on March	No Power	15-110-15-117
8	7264	707	14:01 on March	No Power	15-110-15-143
9	7269	705	14:02 on March	No Power	15-110-07-210
10	7268	708	14:02 on March	No Power	15-110-15-114
11	7271	709	14:02 on March	No Power	15-110-07-221
12	7270	706	14:02 on March	No Power	15-110-02-139
13	7272	705	14:03 on March	No Power	15-110-07-218

The Trouble Call Analysis engine looks for spatial patterns and relationships between the calls and the transformers known to be down. This dialog box allows the user to run an analysis and set a time for the engine to run through its cycle.

Dispatching with great dispatch

A dispatcher using Responder has all of the information generated by the TCA engine, as well as a list of all the original trouble calls, available to her in the Responder client window. She can pan and zoom on a map showing all the trouble transformers, and begin to make some determinations about priorities based on how many homes or businesses are affected by each incident.

In the example seen here, the incidents highlighted in blue on the map are linked to the customers highlighted in black. The red triangles are the transformers (not the customers). A transformer feeds one to ten households, but the assumption (based on experience) in the company is that they'll never get calls from every customer. In this case, six customers have called in, but the system is reporting ninety-six customers affected since that's the total number served by that circuit.

The dispatcher next assigns that incident to a specific service truck known to be available immediately. As crews call in their restoration steps, dispatchers use Responder to open and close devices, switch between circuits, place jumpers, and indicate downed or otherwise affected spans of wire.

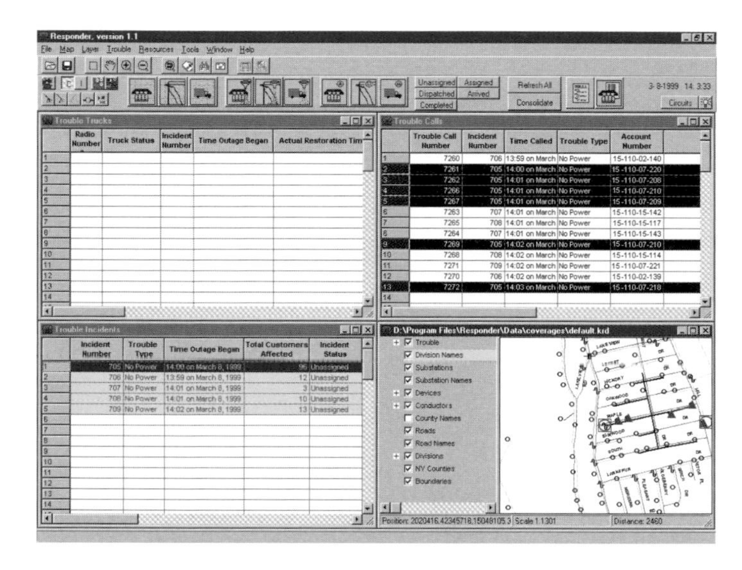

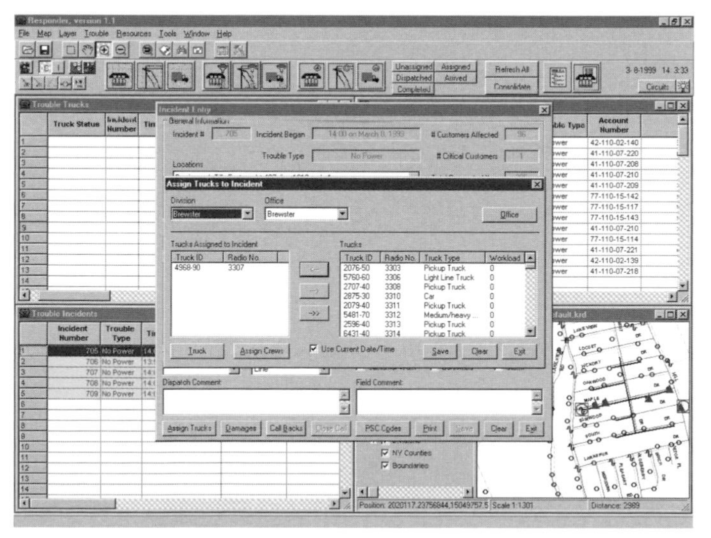

In extreme weather situations like a lightning storm, NYSEG's Responder client application serves as a virtual triage station.

The lights are on again

While crews are out slipping around on the wet roads, managers in the dispatch office examine Responder trouble summary maps, such as the one shown here, to see where functioning circuits are.

This information allows them to determine which neighborhoods have restored power (and therefore which trouble calls can be "tagged" as resolved). To those areas where especially severe damage would require reconstruction or other time-consuming repairs or would prevent prompt restoration of service, managers could often use this same information to help reroute services through functioning transformers.

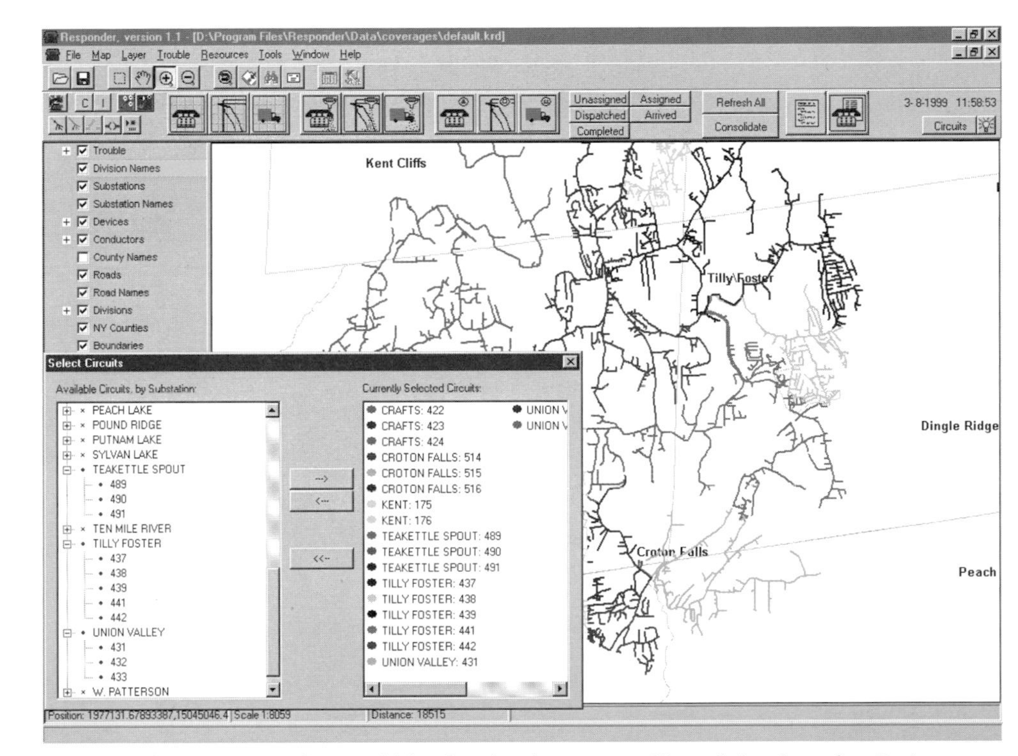

This map colors streets according to which substation they are served by and also shows functioning circuits.

System configuration

NYSEG's Responder application is a classic example of a tightly integrated geographic information system. Information travels freely from one application to the next (and back), meaning that everyone using the system always knows they're working with the most complete and up-to-date information available.

Separate (but connected) databases manage the land base information, facilities information, and trouble incidents.

Each part of the application pulls what it needs at any given moment from the appropriate database and also feeds information back into the databases. There is no data lag time: everyone is seeing everything in real time.

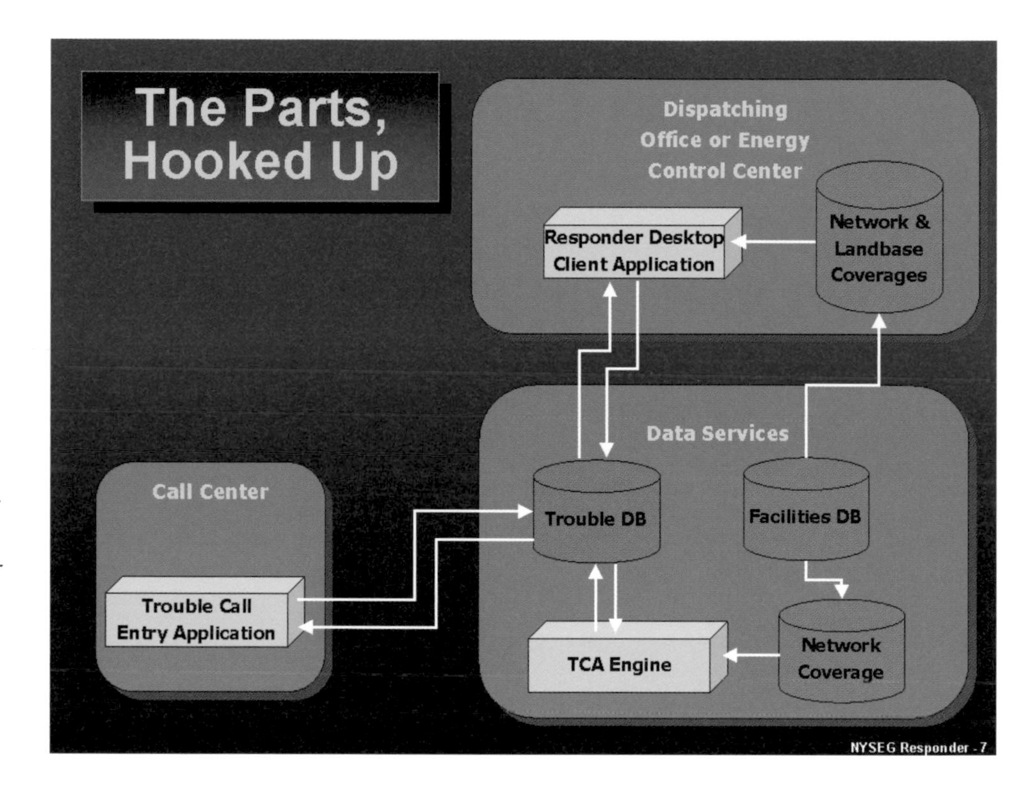

Conclusion

Responder replaced an antiquated, semi-automated trouble ticket system that was labor intensive and unreliable. After an analysis of alternatives, they contracted with Miner and Miner to build a system that uses native ARC/INFO data and a new RuleBase.

The new system is among the most advanced ever deployed at a major utility. In addition to speeding up response time, the system has also given upper managers a tool for monitoring situations as they are unfolding, instead of having to go into the dispatcher's office like they used to.

Hardware

Client machines: Compaq Deskpro 6000 (384 MB RAM, 300 MHz)

Servers: IBM® RS/6000™ AIX® (1.5 GB RAM, four processors per machine, RAID array storage, scalable to 12x12)

Analysis engine server: Compaq R3000 (512 MB RAM, RAID array storage)

Network: 16-MB LAN, 384K frame relay WAN to dispatch centers

Software

ARC/INFO

ArcFM

Spatial Database Engine™ (SDE™)

Acknowledgments

Thanks to Bill Gale, New York State Electric & Gas Corporation.

Chapter 3

Enterprise GIS

The utility industry is about to emerge from the safe haven of a regulated market to a highly competitive deregulated market, dramatically changing the way utilities operate and serve customers. In the same way that an open market caused telephone companies to seek innovative solutions, utility professionals are now looking at information technology to help them operate as efficiently as possible.

In this chapter, you'll learn about a major utility in Texas that uses GIS applications across its entire enterprise, and you'll see two of these applications at work—a program for managing pole attachments and another for fulfilling call-before-you-dig requests.

Reliant Energy HL&P

Reliant Energy HL&P, formerly Houston Lighting & Power, placed its first arc light into operation in 1882, just three months after Thomas Edison directed completion of the nation's first central station electricity-generating plant in New York City.

Today, more than one hundred years later, HL&P serves over 3.7 million people in the 5,000 square miles surrounding Houston, Texas. This area, only about 2 percent of the state of Texas, accounts for almost a third of the state's consumption of electricity.

Getting power to all these people requires a staggering array of equipment including thirteen power-generating plants, thousands of miles of distribution and transmission lines, and some three-quarters of a million power poles.

Since becoming electrified in 1882, Houston, Texas, has grown from a sleepy town of 20,000 on the bayou to the fourth-largest city in America.

The business of pole attachments

Any sort of equipment placed on a power pole is referred to in the industry as a pole attachment. Until fairly recently, about the only attachments that you would see on a power pole (besides the power company's equipment) belonged to the telephone company. Legislation dating back to the 1930s strictly regulated how these pole attachments were handled and how much the local phone company could be charged for them.

But in the 1980s the wired revolution took off and a host of new communications services began seeking space on the poles to deliver their services. And in the 1990s, cable television providers, cellular phone services, and Internet services all began clamoring for space on the poles. To ensure fair competition, Congress modified the regulations for pole attachments to include these other types of telecommunications providers.

While utilities may have been displeased at being forced to accept pole attachments from others, these new rules also allowed them to contract with the companies who wished to lease space on the poles.

Space on power poles in large cities is often leased by other companies for cable TV, wireless, and local telephone services. With tens of thousands of poles often controlled by a single utility (like HL&P) and with multiple leases on each pole, the logistics of managing this part of this business is best handled with geographic information technology.

Managing the leases

Reliant Energy HL&P owns 750,000 power poles. Just keeping track of the poles themselves, let alone the different leases on each pole, is a huge task that is ideally suited for a geographic information system.

The location of each pole is stored in the HL&P master ARC/INFO database, along with many other layers of data including streets and highways, homes and businesses, and information about the rest of the infrastructure.

To manage the increasingly complex job of pole attachment leases, HL&P developed a custom ARC/INFO application so that people who don't know GIS can access the database.

The application features a map interface and a query menu that allows the selection of all the poles leased by a certain company. In the example seen at the right, the white dots represent poles leased by a local cable television firm. The red circles represent poles owned by HL&P but not leased to anyone.

This screen shows the interface used to select all the poles that have space leased to a particular company. The white dots represent poles with cable television equipment attached.

Saving time

The people at HL&P who manage the lease agreements have come to rely on the system and can't believe they used to do the work without it. GIS managers at the company are convinced that the success of the application is due to its ease of use.

When a car crashed into a pole at the intersection seen on the map at the right, HL&P work crews needed to replace the pole. Before they could bring the damaged pole down, they needed to notify the other companies with equipment on the pole so those companies could get to the scene and reroute their services.

An employee in the right-of-way department got the accident call. He first selected the pole (highlighted in green) by pointing to it and clicking it with the mouse. What he saw next was a list of companies with attachments to the pole. He then clicked on the question mark next to Phonoco to bring up the details of the lease. The company/emergency info button displayed detailed information on the leaseholder, including the person to contact in case of an emergency.

Within moments of the call, HL&P had notified Phonoco and told them what the problem was and where to send the crew.

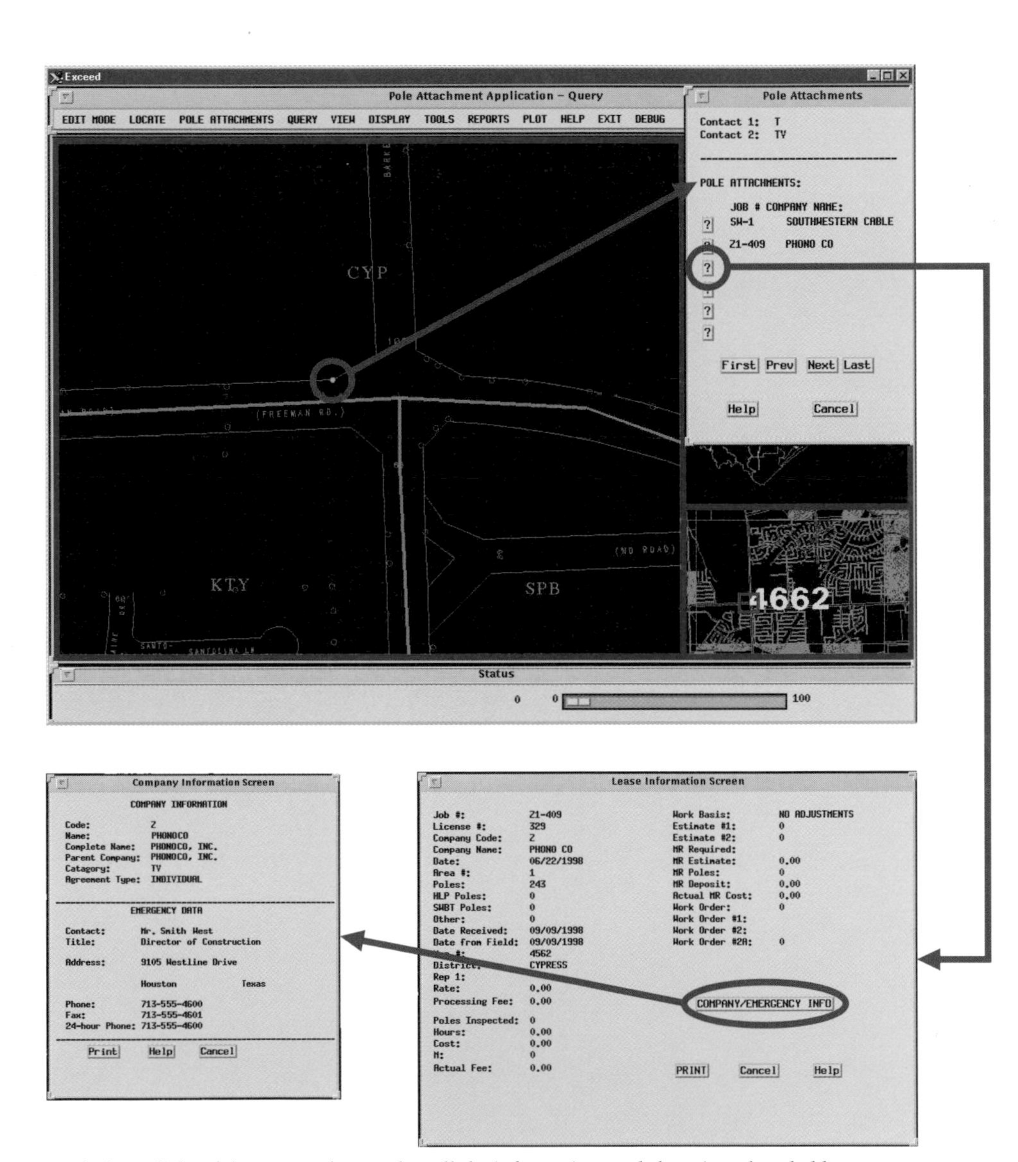

With three clicks of the mouse, the user has all the information needed to give a leaseholder details about an emergency.

Unauthorized pole attachments

Not all attachments are authorized. The majority were placed there before the new regulations came into effect, and before HL&P was actively managing pole attachments by computer.

HL&P crews submit reports when they find questionable attachments in the course of their field work. The GIS department, in turn, updates the database with this information. Managers at the right-of-way department can then initiate lease negotiations with the companies that placed the equipment there in the first place.

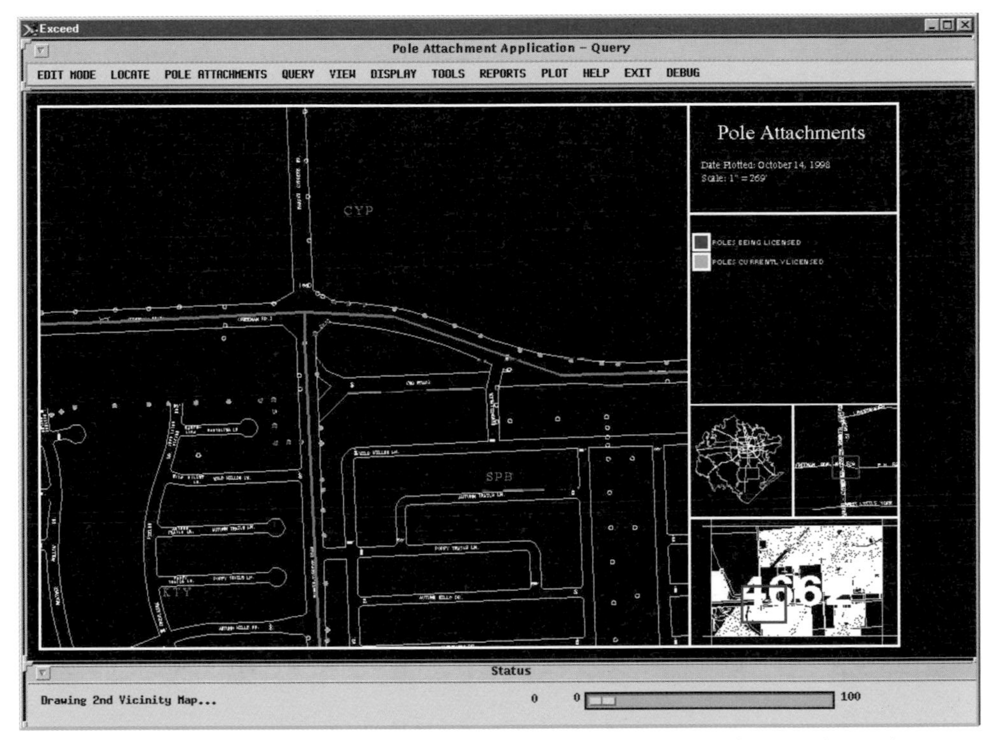

Finding the poles that have unauthorized attachments is a way for HL&P to update its pole attachment leases.

Call before you dig

Every year, power outages, disrupted phone service, broken gas lines, environmental messes, serious injuries, and even death result when people who think they know what's buried under their property begin excavating without first checking with their local utilities. To prevent such accidents, systems have been established so that everyone from professional contractors to weekend builders can identify underground facilities before they lean into their shovels.

In Texas, as in most states, it's the law: before a homeowner or contractor can break ground for a home addition, swimming pool, fence, or other project that requires excavation, they must make sure they're clear of all underground utility lines.

In Texas, people can call a toll-free number to report where they plan to excavate. The information is passed on to the appropriate gas, telephone, electric, or water utility. HL&P gets about a thousand such calls a day. Their GIS-based tool for researching dig requests has saved the company hundreds of thousands of dollars annually and significantly reduced incidents like those pictured at the right.

The dangers of not calling before you dig are self-evident in these pictures.

Photos courtesy of *Underground Focus* magazine

GIS without maps

Most GIS applications display maps. But there is another type of GIS application in which geographic analysis takes place in the background and no map display is required. HL&P's One-call program is such an application.

Here's how it works: records for each call to the One-call center are transmitted electronically as ASCII files to HL&P throughout the day and are loaded into HL&P's master database.

The ARC/INFO application runs twenty-four hours a day, address matching each record to its parcel database. If it locates an exact match (which it almost always does), the program then checks other layers of HL&P infrastructure data and creates a report of underground facilities HL&P has at or near that address.

While human beings still review the results, this first round of automated research saves time and speeds up the utility's response.

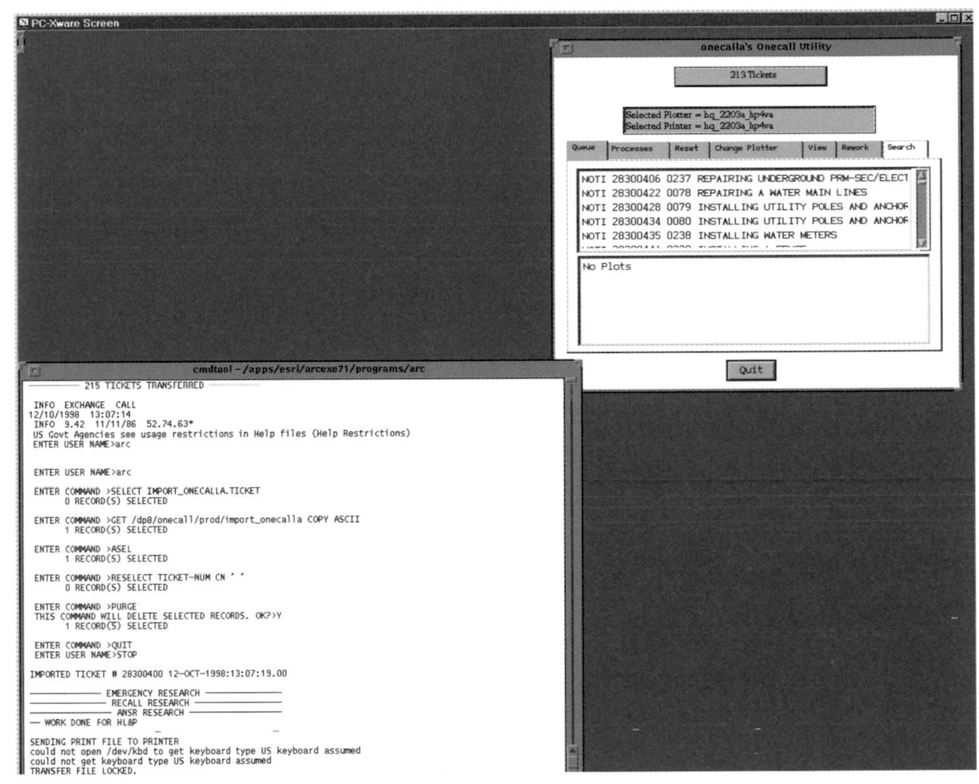

Although there's no map to be seen, a powerful ARC/INFO application is at work researching hundreds of call-before-you-dig requests.

Where *not* to dig

The question with each call is "Do we need to send someone out to the job site to mark the location of HL&P facilities?" The ARC/INFO program makes the first attempt at a decision. It's able to eliminate up to half the calls in which an exact address match is made and no HL&P facilities are found on the premises.

For the rest, HL&P staff must do some additional research. Geographic information managers have created a set of tools that makes this job easier, too.

For example, staffers can peruse all tickets electronically and bring up a digital map of the area to see what's there. If they establish that there is in fact equipment buried there, they can mark or circle the exact location and send out a detailed map with the crew on the following day.

Before the GIS was implemented, the staff had to dig through drawers of printed maps and order copies for the field crews. The automated system allows them to do most of the work directly on their computers.

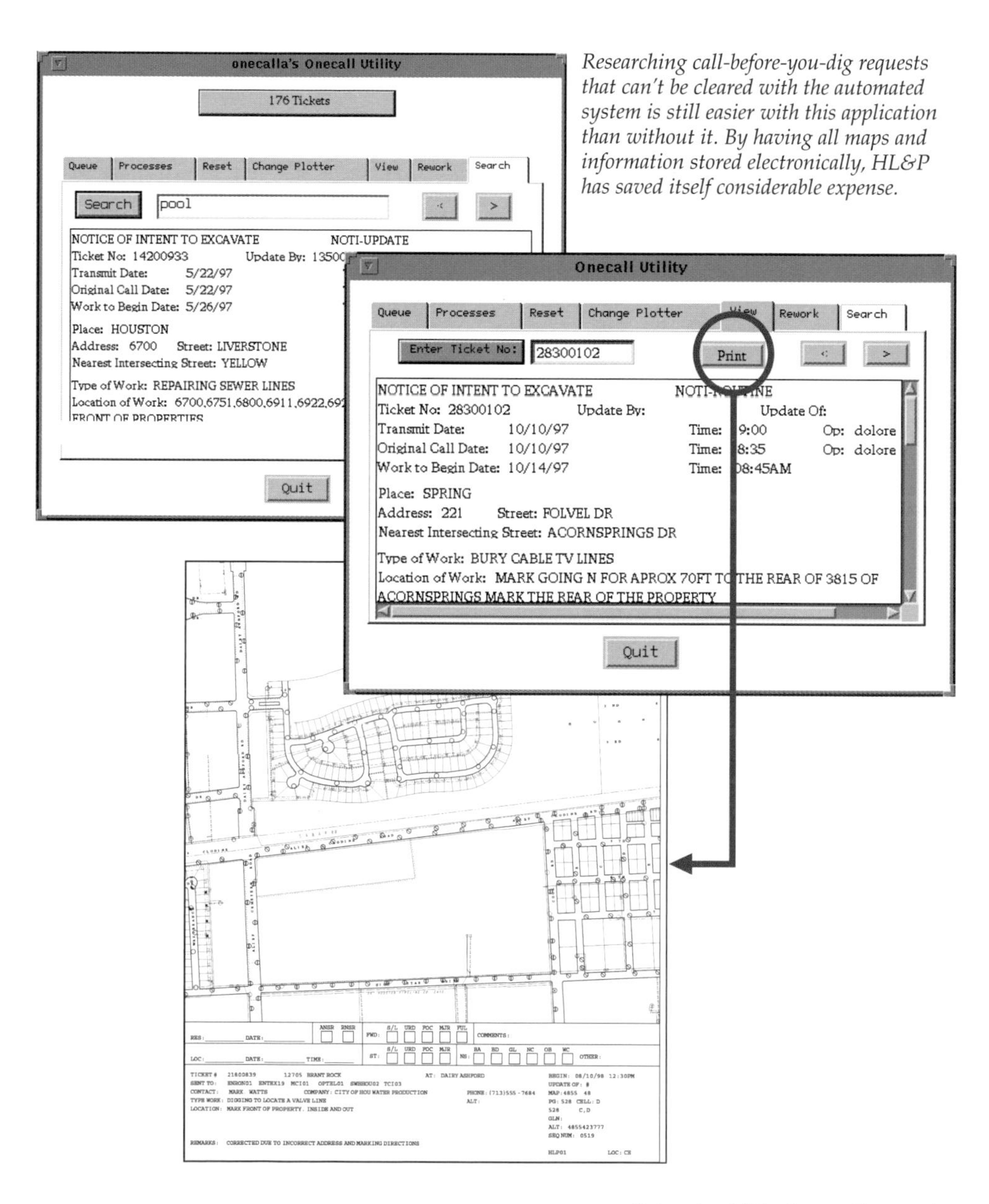

Researching call-before-you-dig requests that can't be cleared with the automated system is still easier with this application than without it. By having all maps and information stored electronically, HL&P has saved itself considerable expense.

Out of the file cabinet

After providing information to the contractor or homeowner—flags or spray-painted lines showing where not to dig—the field person comes back with information, notes about the project, and details about what was marked on-site.

Initially, there was no way to get this information into the database short of having a GIS or database technician sit down and manually edit the record. This procedure was time-consuming and inconvenient.

Eventually, a better solution was found, and crews were sent out with laptop computers. Instead of marking what they did on a map printout, they entered the details into the laptop, and then uploaded the information to the database in the office.

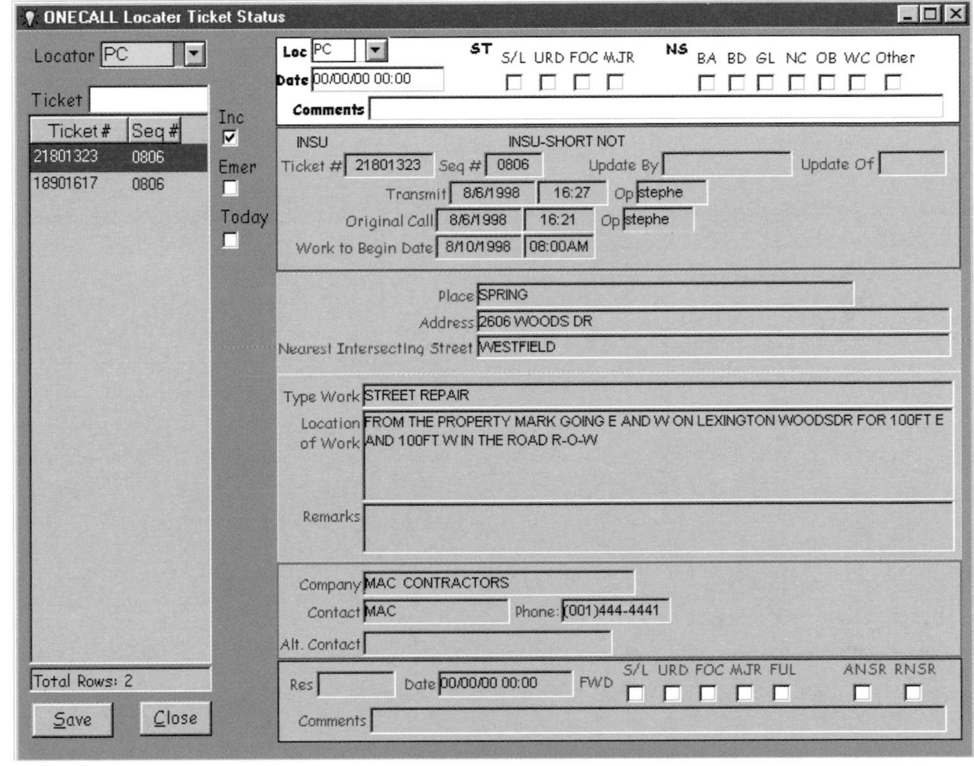

This is the screen that the field technicians see on their laptop computers. It allows them to look at the job tickets for a given day, and enter details about particular tickets into the computer.

Conclusion

These two applications represent only part of the value Reliant Energy HL&P gained by using GIS. As business users within the company define new needs for spatial data, GIS programmers work with them to make their requirements a reality. This process model provides increasing benefits far in excess of costs, and allows the use of GIS data to be integrated into every aspect of HL&P's utility business.

The system

The pole attachment and One-call applications are just two of many enterprise GIS applications deployed by Reliant Energy HL&P. They are running ARC/INFO version 7.1.2. The ARC/INFO data is managed in ARC/INFO LIBRARIAN™ and resides on the primary data server, a Sun™ SPARCcenter™-2000. Additionally, a Sun Ultra™ Enterprise™ 4000 server hosts X sessions for GIS users who run Hummingbird™ Exceed® version 6.0 software on their PCs to create the X sessions.

The pole attachment tables containing tabular lease and company information are in INFO™ software. The application is written in ARC Macro Language (AML™) software.

Acknowledgments

Thanks to Jeff Myerson, Janice Powell, David Bishop, and Richard Klapper of Reliant Energy HL&P.

Chapter 4

From the rubble of war

It's challenging enough to manage an electric distribution utility in a big American city that's not even two hundred years old and has never seen a war. But to manage the power needs of a city five thousand years old and bomb-scarred after sixteen years of civil war means coping with damaged infrastructure and chaotic redevelopment, not to mention thousands of connections to the system that aren't being paid for.

In this chapter, you'll read how an ambitious program undertaken by the state-run Lebanese electric utility in Beirut has successfully used GIS technology to model the electrical system of their ancient city, and how this effort has helped solve some of the unique problems in distributing electricity in the Middle East.

The city that wouldn't die

Electricité du Liban generates, transports, and distributes power to more than one million customers throughout Lebanon—a nation still rebuilding from the devastation wrought by its sixteen-year civil war.

In Beirut, particularly, EDL's distribution system took a severe pounding during the war. To complicate matters, general lawlessness during wartime followed by chaotic redevelopment resulted in countless illegal connections to the EDL system.

When the war ended in 1992, EDL embarked on an ambitious plan to rebuild the nation's utilities, starting in Beirut with a new geographic information system called GISEL to model and manage the electric infrastructure.

Courtesy of Maps Geosystems

The city of Beirut juts into the Mediterranean. The largest port in the region is located near historic Beirut (circled); both areas are part of a major reconstruction plan.

Transforming the utility

At a time when electric service was a rarity in the country, GIS sounded like a luxury. But managers at EDL were determined to rethink the entire business and transform the utility into a modern, competitive enterprise. This meant having access to the latest information management technology.

Using data digitized from a centuries-old accumulation of paper maps and records, plus new data acquired digitally in the field and through remote (satellite) sensing, EDL and engineering firm Khatib & Alami built a comprehensive GIS database. Included in the database were high-voltage transmission facilities, local distribution equipment, generating plants, natural land features, land use demarcations, and, in short, all the data related to running a modern electric utility. Topology and connectivity have been fully maintained in the database to ensure adequate modeling and simulation of the electric system.

Once the database was completed, a GIS team within EDL then developed a series of applications designed to provide better services to their customers at lower prices, and also to help EDL operate its business according to modern methods.

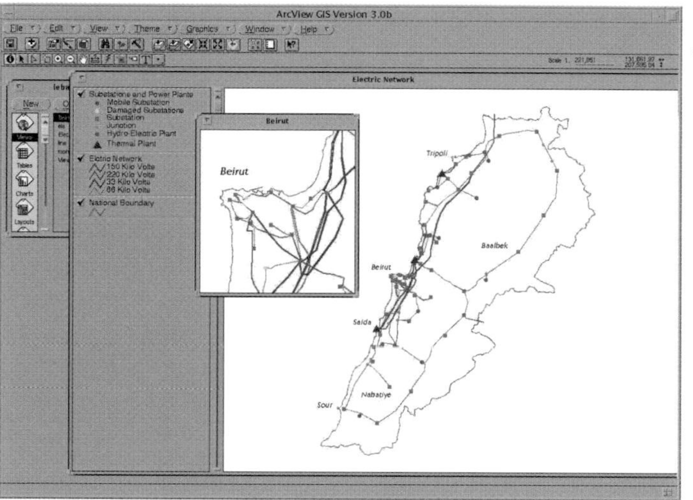

These two maps, made from data stored in the GISEL database, show the nationwide transmission system of Lebanon (left) and the municipal Beirut electric distribution system (below).

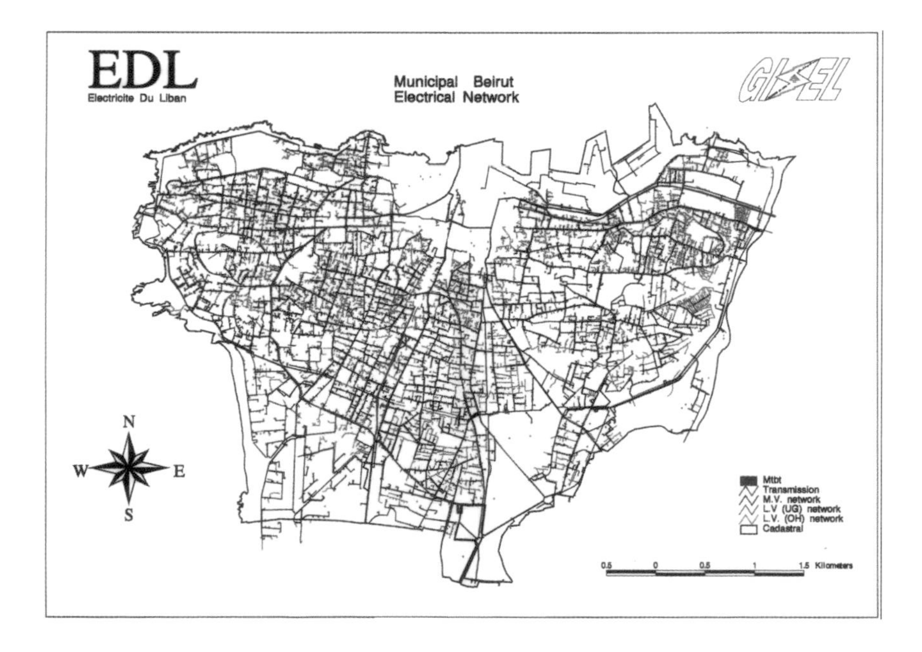

Powering the new construction

So complete was the devastation after the war that much of the rebuilding involved starting from scratch.

Facilities managers at EDL use the application seen at the right to design and document the construction of new substations, transformers, power poles, and other parts of the system. Because they are working directly in the database, changes they make to the system can be easily integrated into the database once they are approved.

Before the GIS database, they had to do this work by digging out the paper records, visiting the site, marking the plans with new constructions, and then redrawing the entire plan.

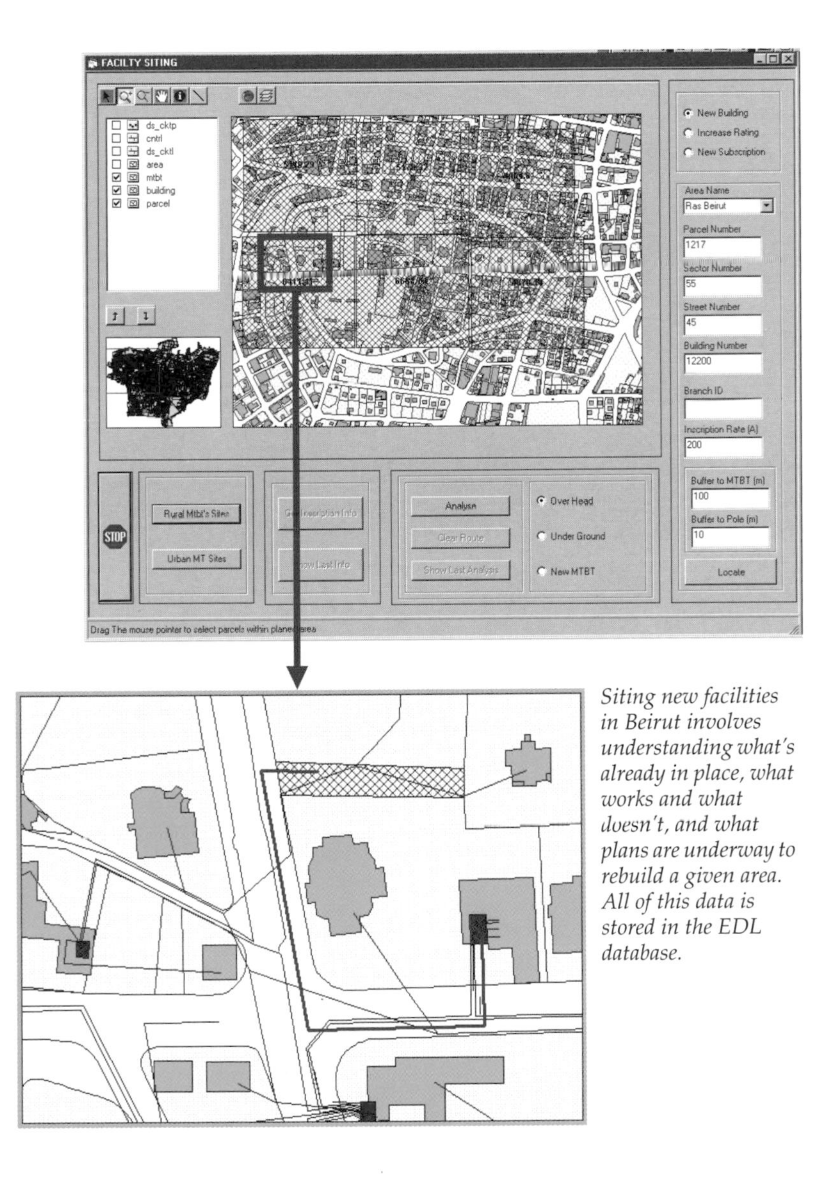

Siting new facilities in Beirut involves understanding what's already in place, what works and what doesn't, and what plans are underway to rebuild a given area. All of this data is stored in the EDL database.

Testing and measuring load capacity

As newly built equipment was connected to equipment that had survived the war, extensive analysis of the system was required to determine the exact capacity (total possible electric load) of the system.

Their Power Flow and Fault Analysis application allows EDL to study loads and faults in the system. The application links traditional schematic maps with spatial representations of the system to create a hybrid model of the information from the same data.

This allows engineers to work from either a true spatial representation or a straight schematic representation as appropriate to the task at hand. The system can even combine the two models into a "quasi-spatial" representation that incorporates schematic-type information in a layout that roughly approximates the true layout of the geography.

Another benefit of the hybrid model (a potential future substitute for schematic panels in dispatch rooms) lies in the fact that it resolves the chronic problem of updating two parallel databases (schematic and spatial). The new schematic model is automatically updated from a single source: the spatial coverage of the distribution network.

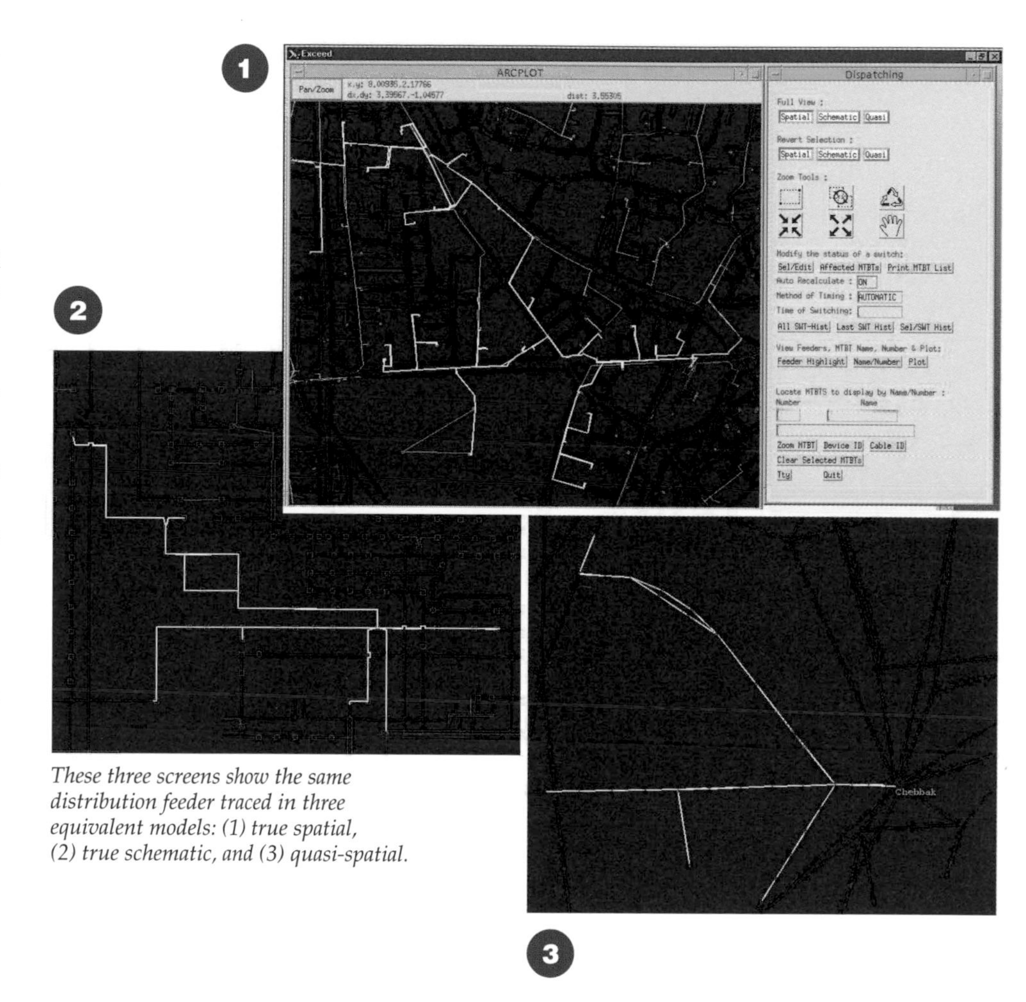

These three screens show the same distribution feeder traced in three equivalent models: (1) true spatial, (2) true schematic, and (3) quasi-spatial.

Pirated power

After the war, EDL had to identify and map all connected users of EDL power to help improve customer service, improve outage management analysis and response, monitor EDL's facilities, and find and eliminate pirated connections.

To do this, they mapped out at the transformer level exactly how much power was being used and how much was being billed and collected.

By carefully analyzing which buildings are being fed by which transformers and comparing the billed usage to actual usage, electricity piracy and losses due to defective equipment are gradually being reduced.

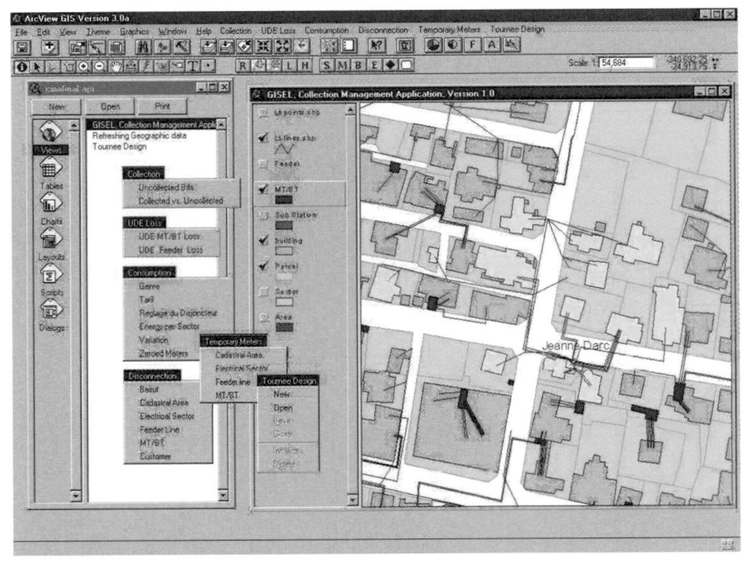

This view shows an application developed by EDL to help collections managers determine who was paying for power and who needed to be billed.

The pie chart at the left represents the problems faced by EDL after the war: only a bit more than half the power from a certain transformer was being paid for. The rest was either billed but not collected, or lost as a result of a technical glitch.

A framework for cooperation

The GISEL project has done more than just make EDL a more responsive and competitive utility. It has also ushered in an era of cooperation in many areas of government, business, and education.

By making data and experience available to other organizations within Lebanon, EDL has helped many of these organizations jump start their own GIS programs.

Adequately furnished, and equipped with the most modern GIS hardware, software, and communication systems, the GISEL facilities, staffed with qualified GIS utility specialists, stand today as a model enterprise GIS facility.

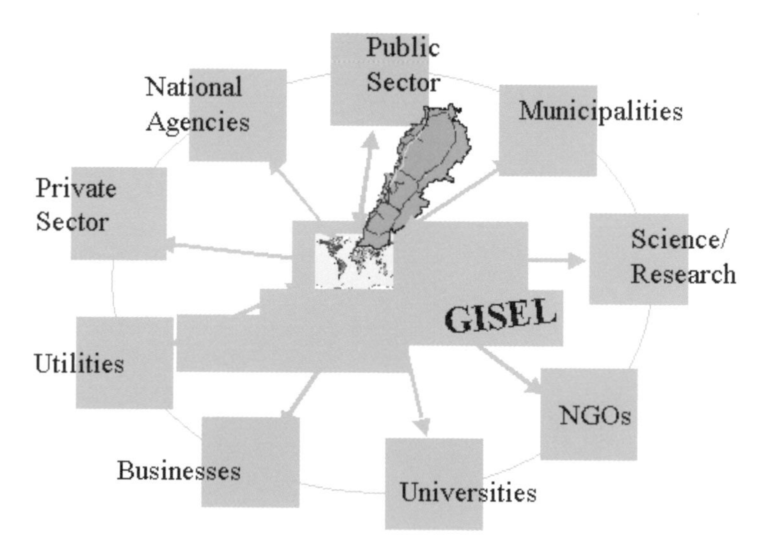

Conclusion

The GISEL project is ongoing. The GIS data model is functional for municipal Beirut and soon will be for greater metropolitan Beirut as well. Once Beirut is complete, work will begin on the rest of Lebanon. Today, GISEL is widely recognized as a pioneering enterprise utility GIS. Its success is being copied in other parts of the Middle East.

Hardware

Application server: Sun Enterprise 450 with RAID

Data servers: Digital™ Alpha™ 4000 (2x266), Sun Enterprise 3000 (2x250), and Microsoft® Windows NT® (Pentium® II, 2x300) with RAID

Terminals: Workstations and PCs (forty)

Peripherals: Plotters, scanners, printers

Software

ARC/INFO for UNIX® and Windows NT

ArcView® GIS version 3.0

SDE server and SDE client

MapObjects®

Extensions: ARC TIN™, ARC NETWORK™, ArcPress™, ARC COGO™

ArcFM

DistOps™

Oracle® version 8.0 server

Oracle client Windows NT

Exceed version 6.0

Applications developed in house

Adhoc, Map Product, Facility Siting, Trouble Call, Work Order, Maintenance, Districting, Collection Management, and Switching

Acknowledgments

Ministry of Hydraulic and Electric Resources

Electricité du Liban

Khatib & Alami—Consolidated Engineering Company

Faculty of Engineering and Architecture—American University of Beirut

Environmental Systems Research Institute, Inc.

Chapter 5

The gas is *on*

Natural gas utilities were among the earliest companies to use spatial information technology for managing their operations. As a consequence, they are finding that their aging mainframe-based legacy systems no longer serve their needs. Rather than bandaging these older systems, many utilities are starting from scratch, which allows them not only to modernize their GIS systems, but also to integrate their spatial databases with their core business databases.

In this chapter, you'll see how a provider of natural gas in western Australia integrated its spatial data into R/3™, the leading enterprise resource-planning software from SAP, and realized immediate and lasting business benefits.

Natural gas, Aussie style

AlintaGas is western Australia's principal supplier of natural gas. Based in Perth, the company purchases natural gas extracted from reserves off the northwest coast of Australia and sells it to homeowners, businesses, and industries.

Almost 400,000 western Australian homes are connected to natural gas, as are seventy-two hundred businesses.

Deregulation of the Australian energy business has led to a market in which AlintaGas competes with electricity, solar energy, wood, and liquid petroleum gas suppliers, as well as other natural gas providers. The company thrives by providing energy at competitive prices and first-rate customer service.

Western Australia, a land of severe contrasts and harsh beauty.

Staying competitive

Managers at AlintaGas realized that their information system was inadequate to compete in the new fast-paced economy of Australia. Besides the fact that it was running on a mainframe actually operated by a competitor, there were also concerns about Y2K reliability. It was time to replace the existing business systems. As an organization that had been using GIS for over a dozen years, AlintaGas needed little convincing that the new system must be spatially enabled at its core.

For their companywide business information system, AlintaGas acquired SAP™ R/3 software running atop a relational database management system from Oracle. As for the spatial component, GIS would no longer exist as an information island—GIS functionality was to be tightly integrated with the R/3 system. To achieve this integration, AlintaGas chose ArcFM, a suite of GIS back-office and browsing software developed by Miner and Miner (an ESRI® business partner). ArcFM runs on top of ARC/INFO software, a high-end GIS application, and Spatial Database Engine (SDE) software, which allows spatial data to be stored in a standard RDBMS.

The entire project was implemented in about nine months, and by early 1998 AlintaGas was using its new Gas Network Information System (GNIS) for everyday operations in all departments.

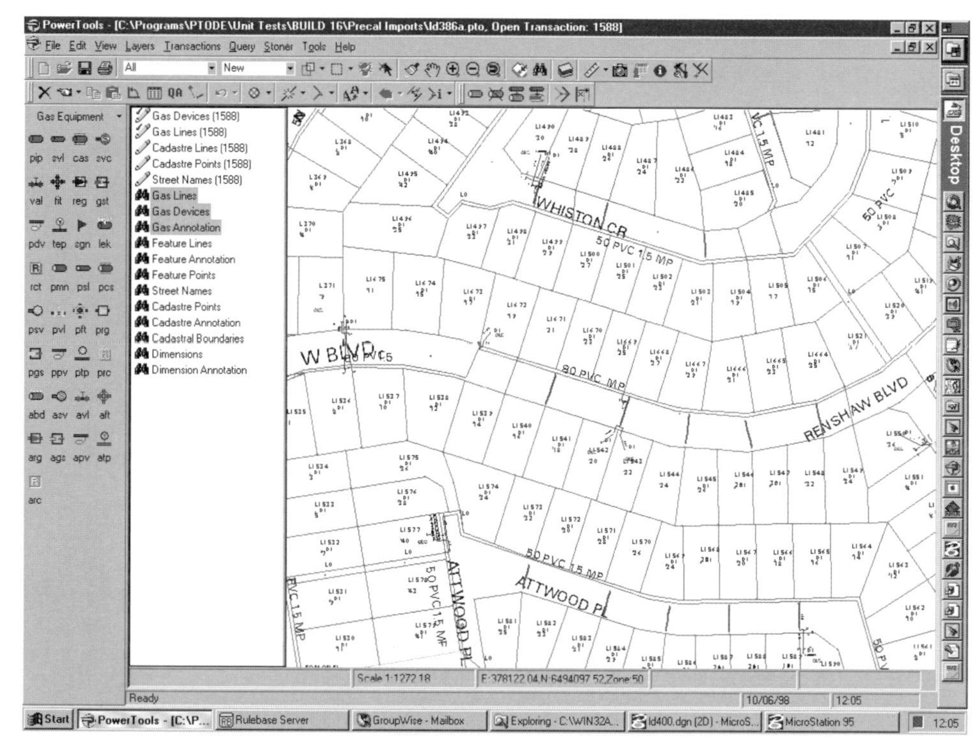

This is the main application interface used by more than one hundred people at AlintaGas. It accesses basic query and navigation tools, as well as advanced GIS applications. Some of the data layers seen here include gas lines and fixtures, property boundaries, and streets.

Navigating the database

GNIS includes a number of navigation tools that make it easy for people to get to the information they need, regardless of their task or GIS skills. These include basic pan and zoom controls that virtually anyone who has used a computer will find intuitive, as well as an identify tool that allows someone to pull up attributes about any feature on the map simply by pointing at it.

In addition to the tools that work directly on the map screen, there are also ways to access data by attribute. The Address Search, for instance, allows employees to locate a customer who has called in with a service problem by typing in an address or phone number. The map then automatically pans and zooms to that location. Once the customer's property is shown in close-up on the map, employees can turn on additional layers and use the identify tool to determine what equipment is located there. Moreover, they can pull up detailed maintenance records that might help diagnose the problem.

An engineer looking at the same problem might use the Query Builder to highlight all equipment of a certain type. Because Address Search and Query Builder adhere to commonly used Microsoft Windows® protocols, the time it takes for someone to use these tools is minimal.

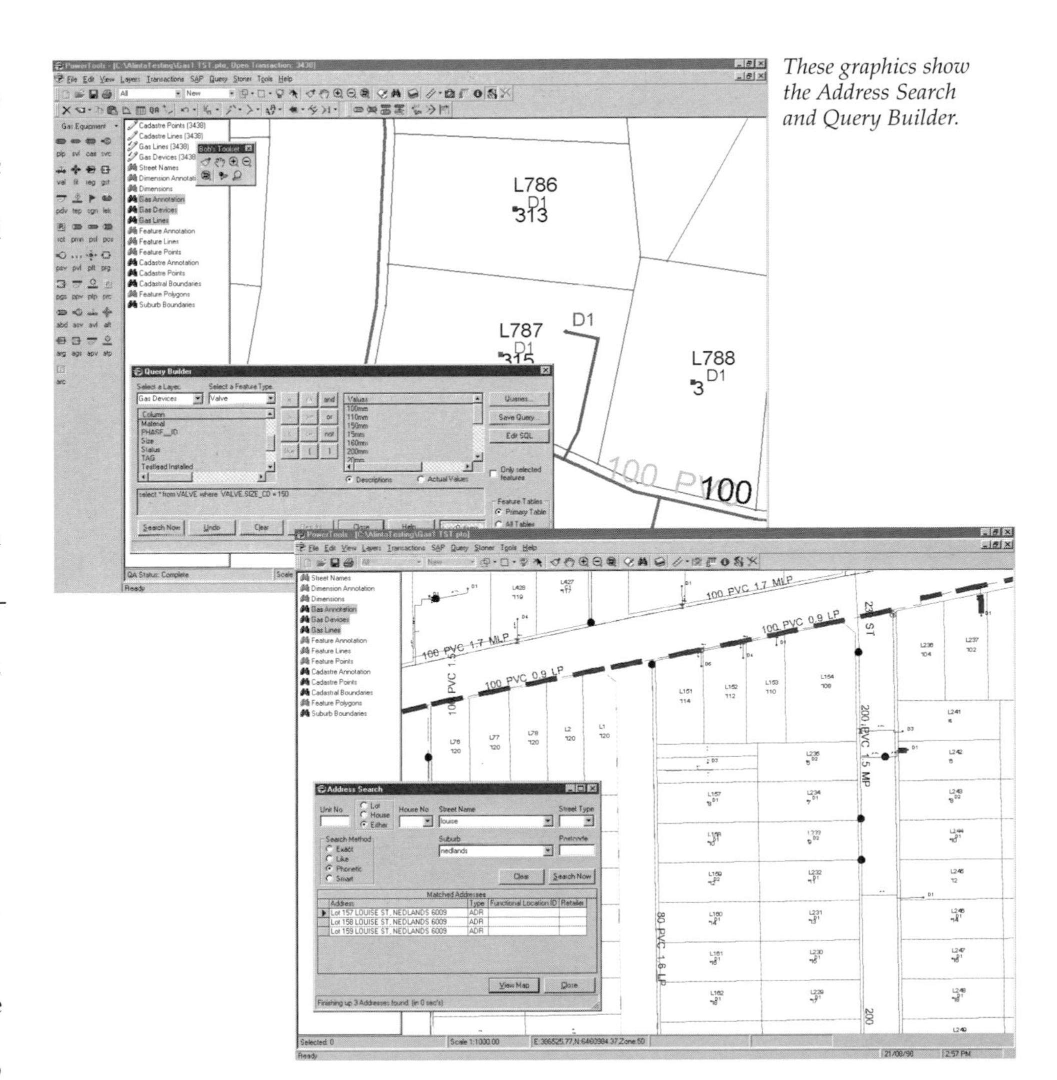

These graphics show the Address Search and Query Builder.

Database editing

The price of an accurate and useful database is eternal maintenance.

Before the GNIS system, changes to the database could only be made by GIS specialists in the Distribution Division of AlintaGas. While these people still make most edits and serve as the "keepers" of the spatial database, many routine updates can now be carried out by other employees.

For example, if a service crew has performed a repair and replaced a section of pipeline on the gas network, an engineer in the department can use the Edit Attributes command to open the database record for that feature and make the edits directly into the table. A set of rules prevents him from making any changes to the record that do not conform to the way that AlintaGas operates the system.

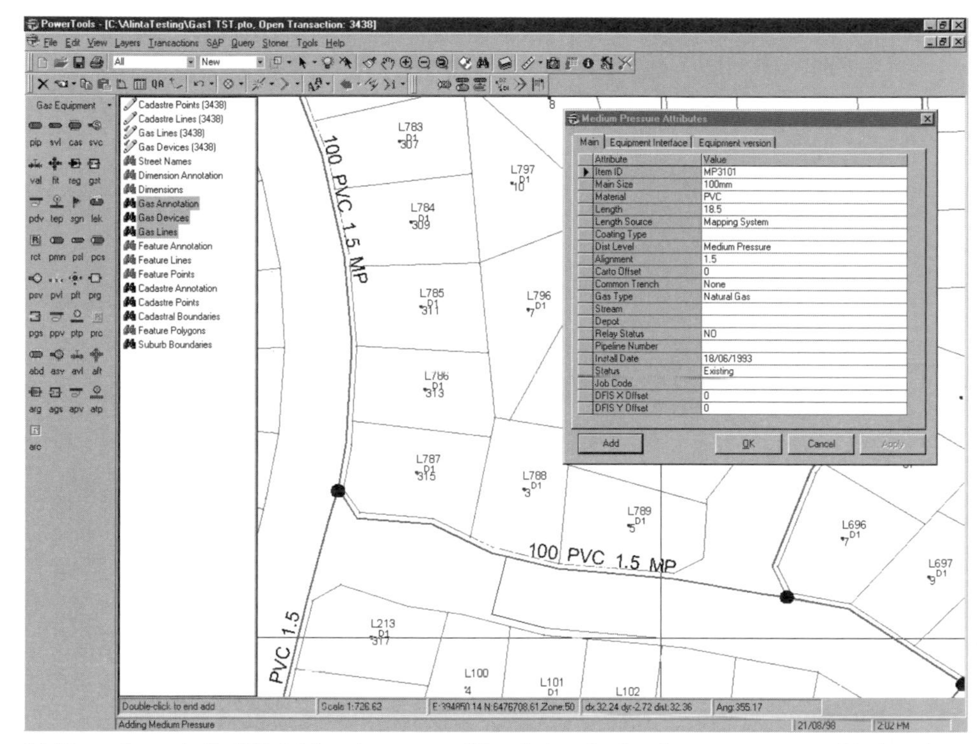

Making a change to the GIS database is now something that can be done by support personnel in just about any department, instead of solely by a GIS specialist after the fact. This makes database maintenance easier (because more people are sharing the load) and faster (because lag times are avoided).

Tracing the network

Perhaps no situation in a natural gas network is as critical as a break in a main gas line. In addition to the obvious danger posed by leaking gas, such a break means that customers will lose service. Using a combination of spatial information technology and good old pipeline know-how, managers at AlintaGas can isolate a break in a gas main and get repair people to the scene in short order.

When a call comes into the AlintaGas nerve center, on-duty personnel must gauge the extent of the problem. Using information about the break supplied by crews at the scene, engineers back at headquarters run a model known as "backgassing" to isolate the service meters affected by the break.

By using the Trace Network command, they can then see the entire path and all of the affected homes. This information can then be radioed to crews in the field.

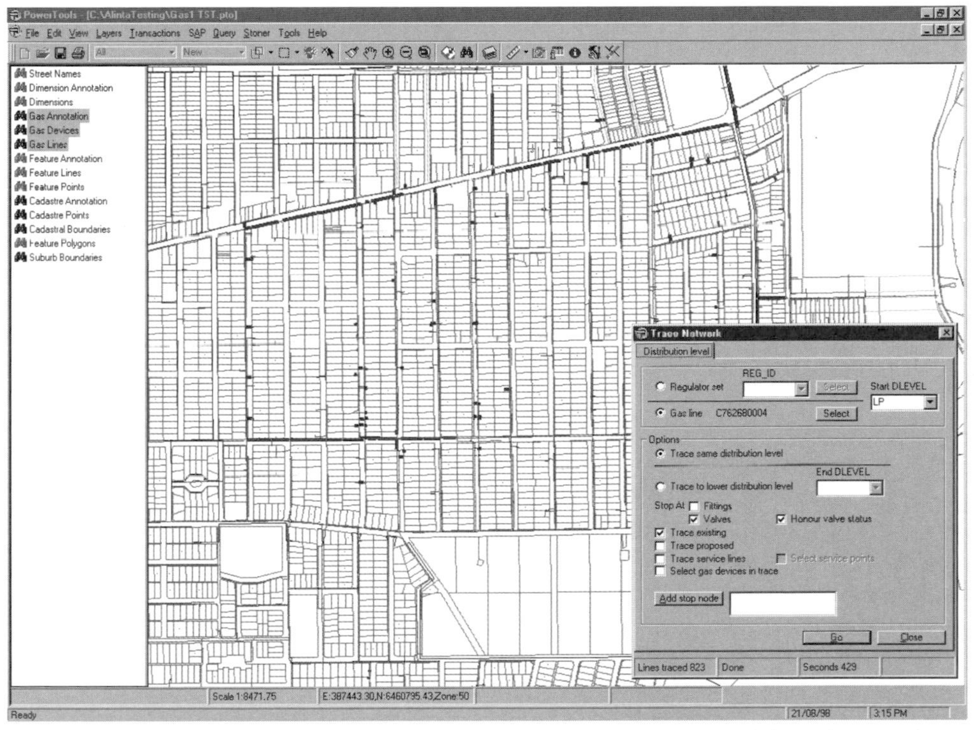

The Trace Network command works on a model of the entire distribution system to help engineers isolate trouble.

The SAP connection

By integrating the GIS system with the SAP R/3 business solution, AlintaGas has increased productivity and reduced the cost of managing data (typically a high cost in a complex utility organization). Instead of having information spread throughout disparate databases, the new system stores all information in two linked Oracle databases: one for the spatial data and one for all the other business data.

Integrating spatial data into the regular business information system has the added advantage of making standard reporting much easier. For example, a manager could go to the map, select a particular neighborhood or suburb by drawing a box around it, then run an ad hoc maintenance report on just that neighborhood. Under the old system, this would have required programming a special report.

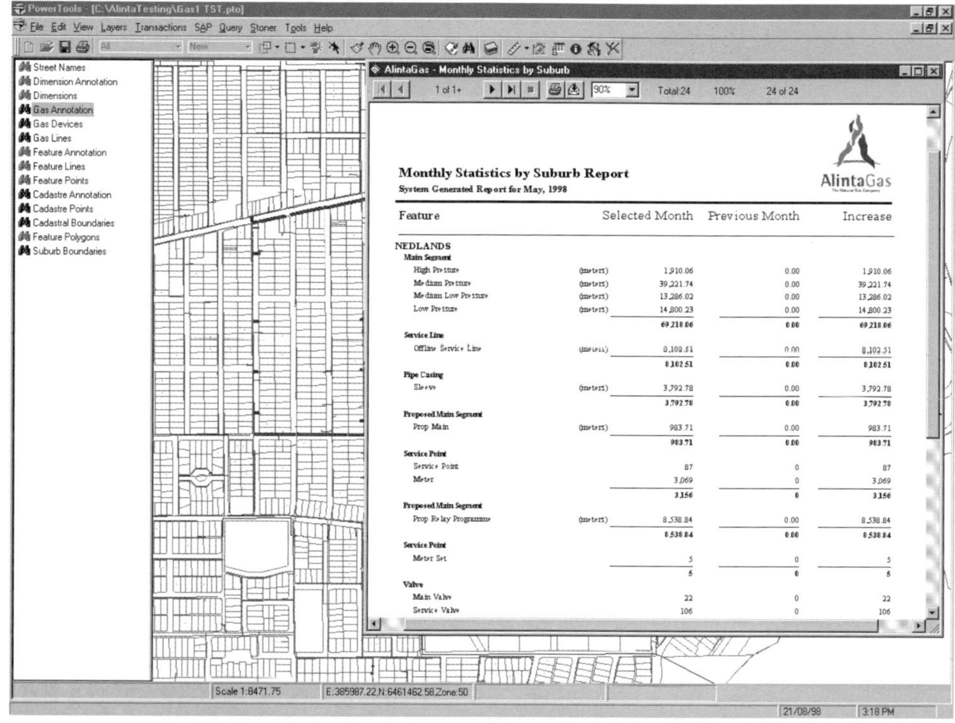

The reporting tool is accessible from a map, allowing managers to create custom reports based on geography.

System architecture

The main server is a Sun machine running Oracle version 7 and the ESRI Spatial Database Engine. The database is about 14 gigabytes, containing map features that represent 11,000 kilometers of gas mains, plus the streets, cadastral parcels, administrative boundaries, and so forth.

All users are connected to the server via a high-speed wide area network.

The engineering and operations departments build, edit, and manage spatial and attribute data using ARC/INFO and ArcFM software. This data can then be viewed and queried by other departments, such as customer service, marketing, and corporate management, with the ArcFM Viewer.

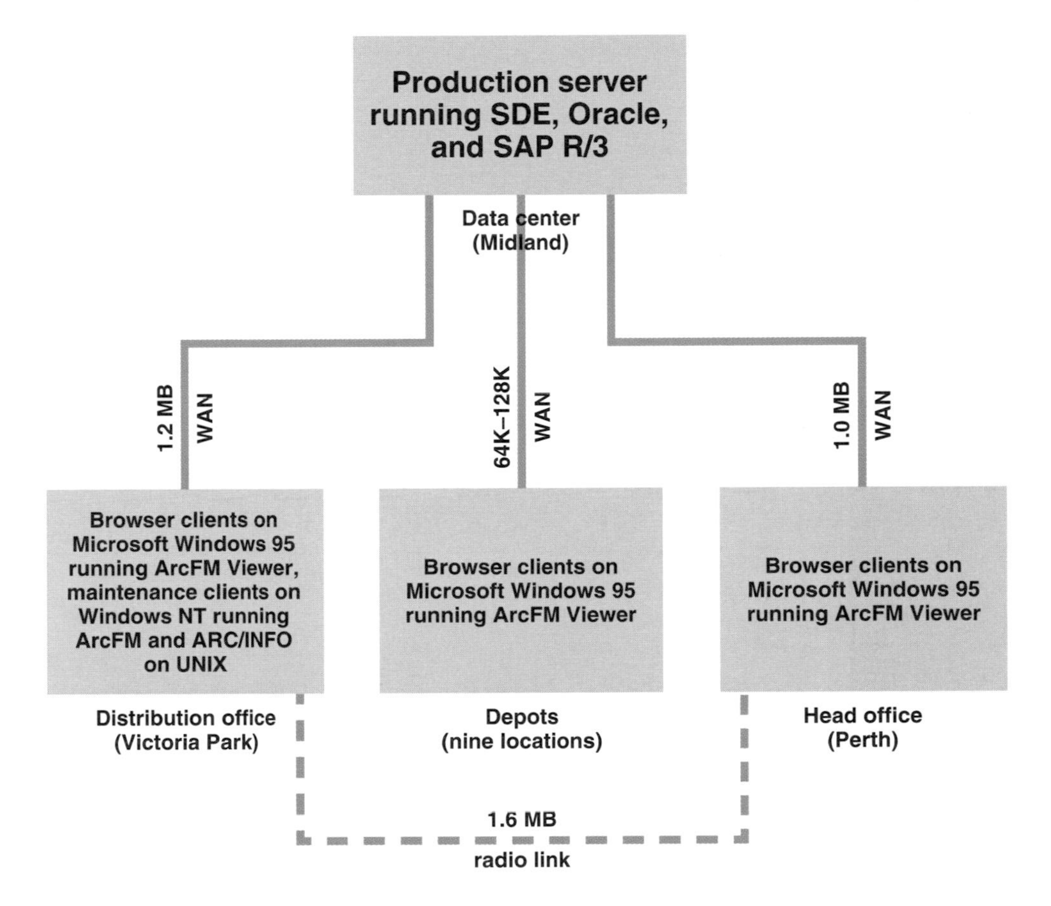

Conclusion

GNIS is operating in a new technology environment that takes advantage of enterprise computing, object-oriented programming, and open hardware, software, and data platforms.

By replacing the previous system, AlintaGas will see the return on its investment in just three years. Phase one of the GNIS and the SAP suite of systems went live at the same time in April 1998 after a rapid implementation. The fast implementation is a testament to the combined efforts of ESRI–Australia and AlintaGas. The overall project (GNIS and SAP) met its major deadline and came in under budget.

GNIS is increasingly being used not just for map representation of the AlintaGas network but also throughout the company as an integral part of day-to-day operations.

AlintaGas has realized its vision of creating an integrated AM/FM system. The key benefits are tight integration at a business-process and system level between the GIS and SAP's enterprise resource-planning software; providing an enterprisewide GIS operating over a WAN on standard office PCs; and providing future strategic business opportunities in areas such as mobile computing, vehicle tracking, and document management.

Hardware

Sun server E-4000

Windows NT clients for ArcFM

Windows 95® clients for ArcFM Viewer

Software

ARC/INFO

ArcFM

ArcFM Viewer

Spatial Database Engine (SDE)

SAP R/3

Acknowledgments

Thanks to Ashok Sharma and Adrian Denning of AlintaGas in Perth, and to David Page, Peter Houwen, and Wayne Hewitt of ESRI–Australia.

Chapter 6

AM/FM: Getting more done for less

To most of us, the initials AM/FM refer to bands in the radio frequency spectrum. But in the electric and gas industries, AM/FM stands for Automated Mapping and Facilities Management, the computerization of mapping for the purpose of operating electric and gas utilities. Automated mapmaking gives managers quick access to information presented in a spatial context. Recent advances in GIS technology have even made it possible to automate the process of designing hookups to new developments.

In this chapter, you'll see how an electric provider in the southeastern United States got its AM/FM GIS system up and running in record time, and how it's used for routine data access as well as automated design.

Responding to deregulation

South Carolina Electric & Gas Company (a division of the SCANA Corporation) is a regulated public utility that generates, transmits, distributes, and sells electricity to wholesale and retail customers, and that purchases natural gas to sell to retail customers. SCE&G serves some 475,000 customers in the southern part of that state.

Strategic planners at SCANA know that the power industry is being gradually deregulated across the country and are positioning their business to compete effectively. The AM/FM system they adopted to address the changing business situation is now used by the whole company.

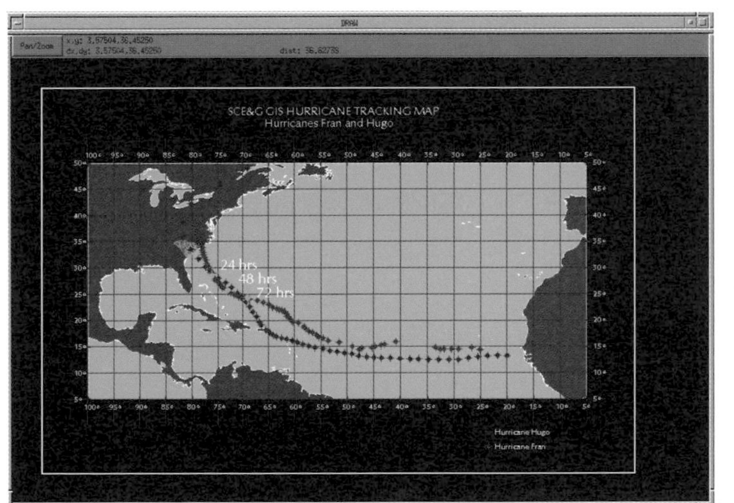

Managing spatially distributed assets is integral to what a power company does. These workers are inspecting transformers that needed to be installed in the wake of Hurricane Hugo.

Rapid implementation

Until the early 1990s, upper management at SCE&G resisted GIS out of skepticism that it could return its cost. But by the early nineties, advances in technology, coupled with plummeting costs, made implementing a geographic information system a natural and obvious choice.

Realizing that a prolonged pilot program would be expensive, technology managers simply jumped in with both feet, getting their very robust system operational in just over a year.

And while a year may sound like a long time, consider that thousands of paper maps had to be converted to digital format, then checked and refined for accuracy.

Once the system was operational, GIS advocates at SCANA were able to produce significant savings in a number of operating areas—most notably in the design of electrical hookups for new residential subdivisions.

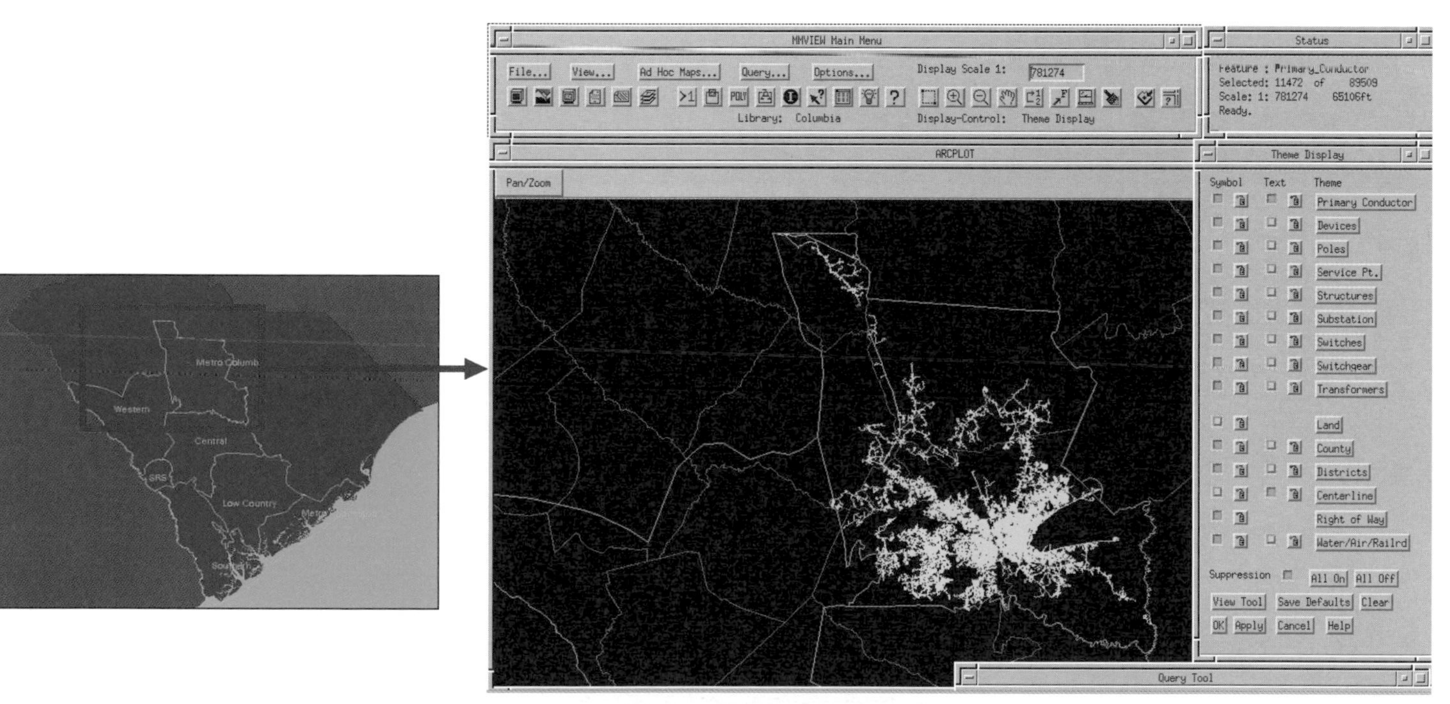

The map at the left shows the state of South Carolina and SCE&G's six electricity districts. The map at the right is an actual screen from the AM/FM system showing the Columbia district. The primary conductors are blue, and the yellow area highlights the conductors within the Lexington local office territory.

What's in the database

An AM/FM database for electric utilities contains both features that are ordinarily visible and those that are buried out of sight.

In addition to layers depicting streets, property lines, and other jurisdictional boundaries, the SCE&G database also includes individual layers containing data about the equipment dedicated to electric distribution—power poles, transformers, underground conduits and cables, fuses, and so forth.

The beauty of having all of these features contained in a single geographically referenced database is that the system designer, emergency response manager, or operations engineer can see everything on the map as the interrelated collection it is. They can decide which layers they want to see according to the task of the moment, whether it's drafting plans for new hookups, planning emergency access routes, or running diagnostic tests on the power system.

The interface to SCE&G's AM/FM system allows people from all over the company to access just the information they need. The map below displays transformers, fuses, reclosers, streets, and poles. Labels for all these features are displayed as well.

Navigating the database

Looking at a map of her district, an operations manager at SCE&G can easily move around the view by panning and zooming. This works fine if she's familiar with the territory and knows exactly what she wants to see. But if she's not sure where something is located, she can also query the database according to a name.

In the example seen on this page, the user has zoomed into the Lake Murray area (depicted on the map as an irregular black shape distinguished by its lack of map features) and then zoomed even farther by selecting Pine Island Drive from a drop-down list.

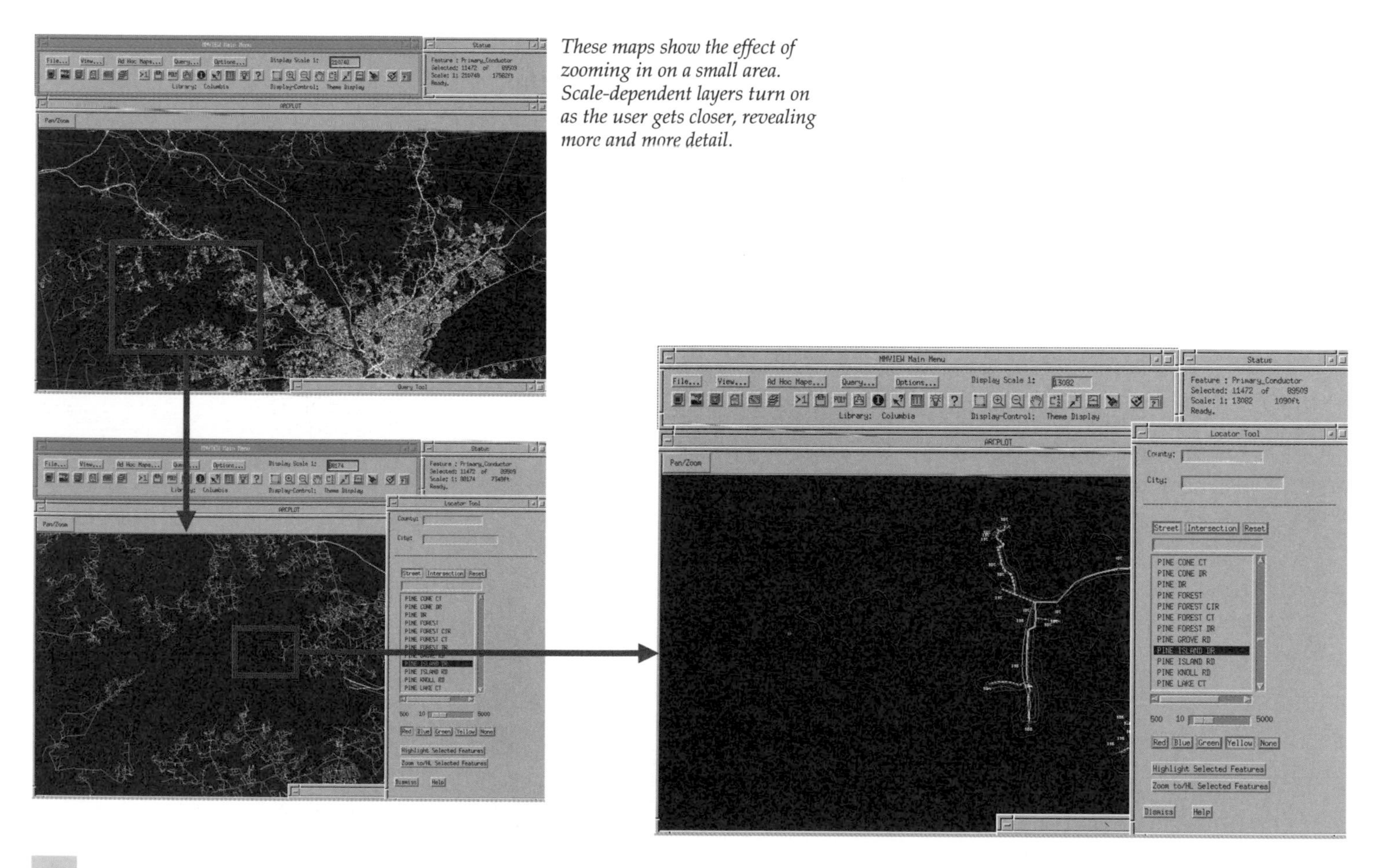

These maps show the effect of zooming in on a small area. Scale-dependent layers turn on as the user gets closer, revealing more and more detail.

Automated mapmaking

Automating the mapmaking process saves money and, just as importantly, gets information more quickly into the hands of those who need it to do their jobs.

It may not seem all that glamorous, but this example shows that the technology has evolved so far that any employee, even those without GIS experience, can create informative and cartographically accurate maps from the GIS database.

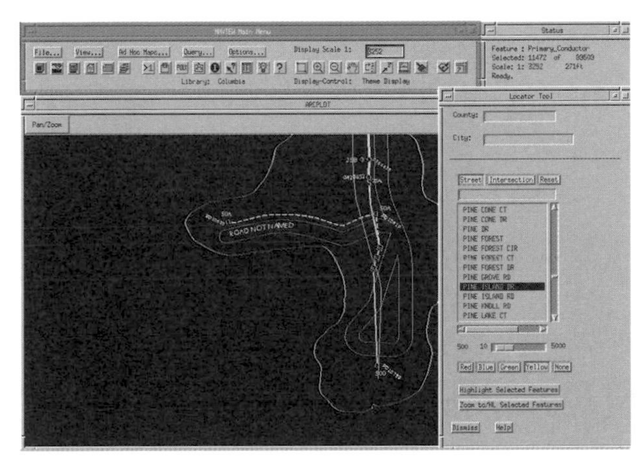

Using wizards (preprogrammed dialog boxes) makes it easy for users at all levels of experience to create usable maps from the SCE&G database.

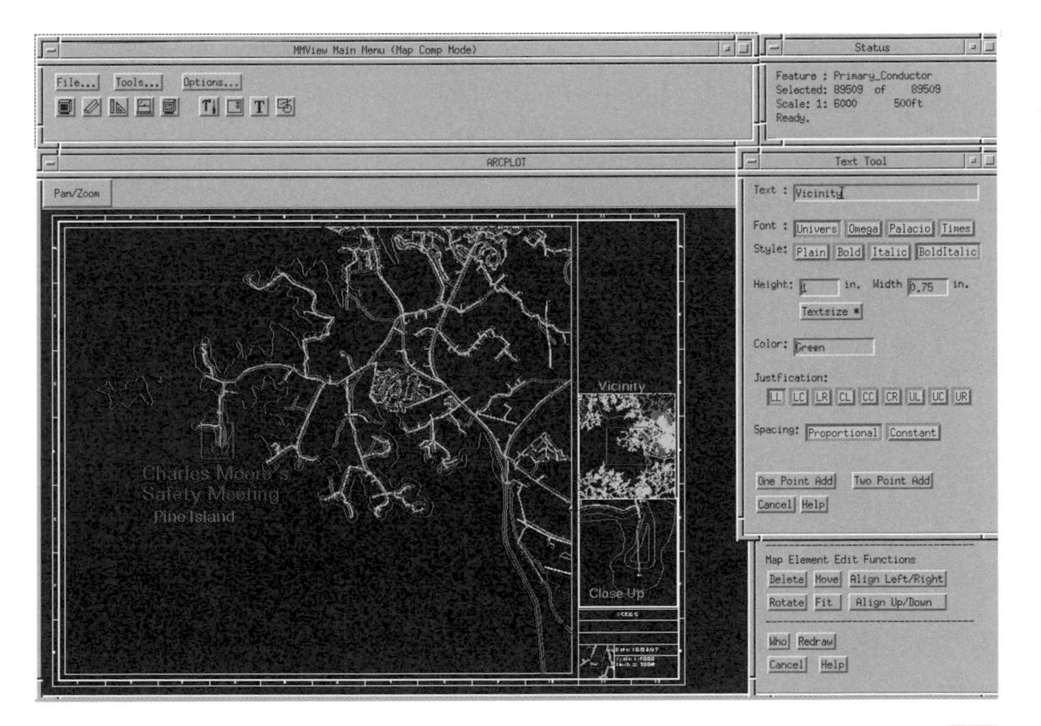

Automated plat design

A more specialized application, but the one that has generated the most well-documented savings, helps engineers design the best way to provide power to new subdivisions.

As a new subdivision is begun, the APD (for Automated Plat Design) takes plans provided by the developer and helps the engineering department create preliminary designs. Alternatives can be quickly evaluated until the designer is satisfied with the configuration. The system is programmed with a set of design rules and practices based on U.S. utility industry standards.

As a result of implementing this system, SCG&E has realized a savings in new construction of approximately 12 percent, which translates into more than a million dollars per year. Design time is reduced from several days to a few hours.

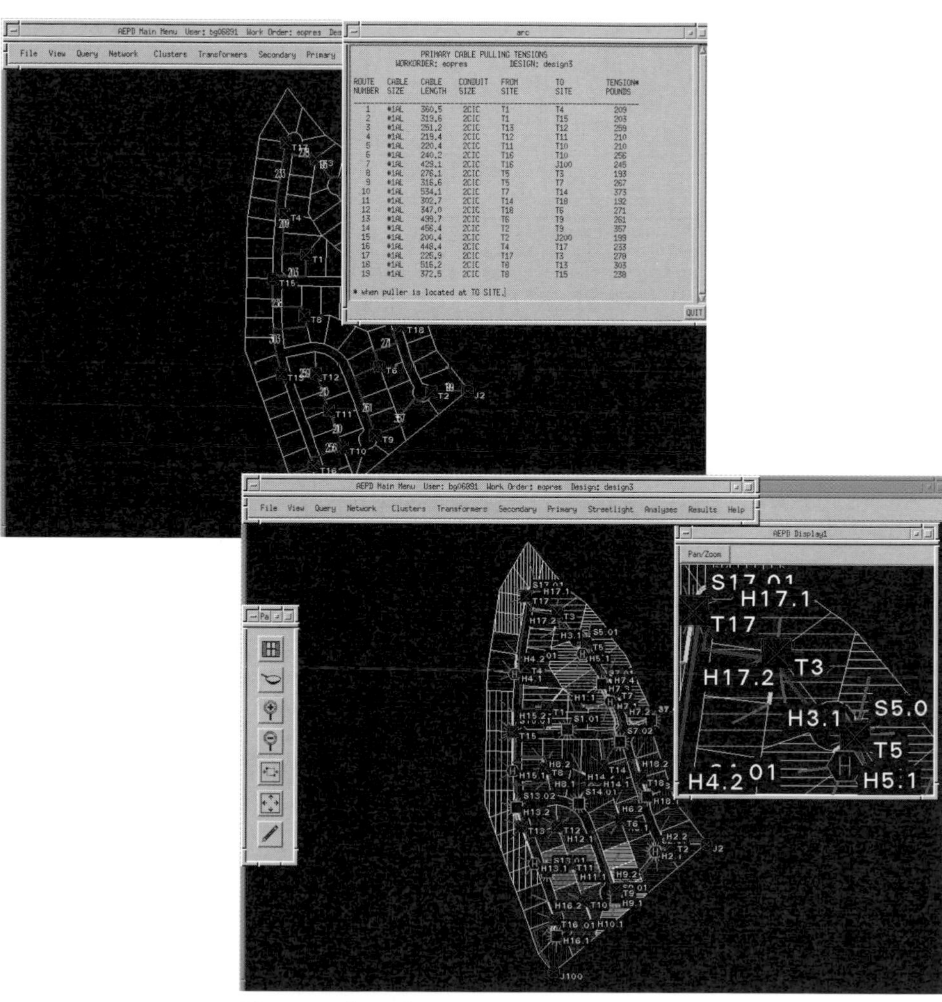

The screen shows the Automated Plat Design interface from Tellus that runs on top of SCE&G's GIS systems.

Conclusion

SCE&G spends about $10 million annually on underground construction related to new developments. Applying the 12-percent figure to this equates to savings of over $1 million a year.

Since implementing GIS and automated plat design, SCE&G has made progress in getting its work order designers to properly use the system and have significantly reduced the cost of construction. At the time of this writing, all medium and large subdivision design work is done with the assistance of the system. Plans are being considered that would move design work even farther into the field as it becomes possible to use the automated system on laptop computers. This should speed up approval and construction even more, while retaining the cost savings that the system makes possible.

Software

Miner and Miner DistOps

PowerTools

ARC/INFO

ArcStorm™

Acknowledgments

Thanks to Chuck Rogers, GIS manager, South Carolina Electric & Gas Company.

Chapter 7

Bolts from the blue

Lightning storms can wreak havoc on power transmission systems. Utilities must not only repair or replace damaged equipment, but often end up paying higher insurance premiums. Of course no utility company can prevent lightning from striking. What they can do, however, is identify the transmission lines and structures most susceptible to strikes and decide whether special shielding equipment or other changes to those lines or structures could help mitigate the impact of direct strikes.

In this chapter, you'll learn how a regional power agency in the Pacific Northwest developed a GIS-based program that analyzes commercially available lightning strike data.

Protecting the grid

Congress created the Bonneville Power Administration, or BPA, in 1937 to market and transmit the power produced at the Bonneville Dam (located west of Portland, Oregon).

Serving nine western states, BPA sells the power from twenty-nine federal dams and one nuclear plant in the Pacific Northwest. The BPA power transmission system is considered one of the largest and most reliable grids in the United States.

The GIS database on which the lightning strike program was built was originally developed to support construction projects and was later used to examine how the hydrosystem would affect threatened and endangered fish runs.

On a summer day, 25,000 lightning strikes is not an unusual number for the Pacific Northwest.

National Lightning Detection Network

To better understand where lightning strikes, Bonneville Power Administration subscribes to a commercial service, the National Lightning Detection Network (NLDN). Using lightning strike detectors strategically positioned across the country, magnetic direction-finding technology, and satellite-based global positioning systems (GPS), NLDN maintains a database of lightning strike locations and intensities that can be downloaded by its clients.

BPA subscribes to data from NLDN that gives the location of the first strike in an event, as well as the "multiplicity," or total number of strikes.

By studying the data, BPA can see where lightning has already struck, and thus predict where it is likely to strike again.

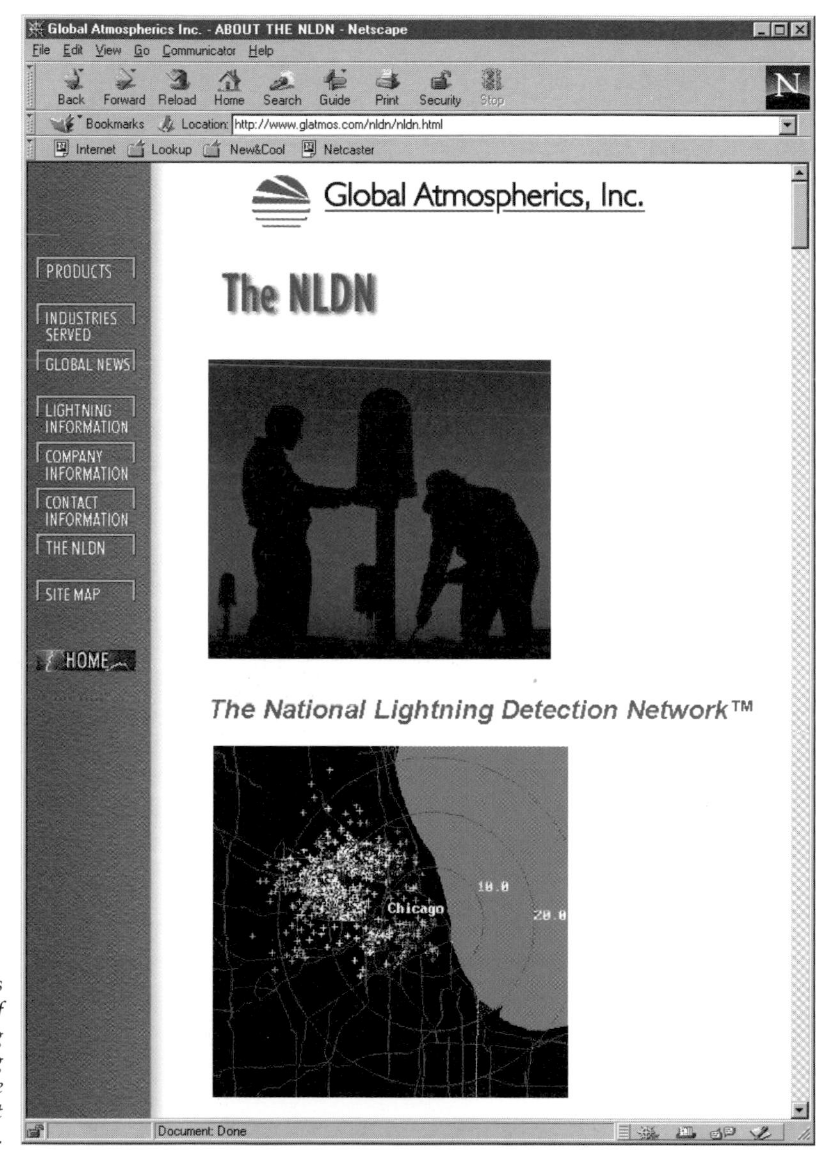

The National Lightning Detection Network's Web site offers information on the science of lightning detection, and has a "Lightning Explorer" that allows anyone to see lightning strikes in real time in their home state. The Lightning Explorer is available at www.glatmos.com/et/et.html.

Finding the strikes that cause outages

Correlating lightning strikes with power outages is a problem of time and space—a natural fit for GIS. To make use of the NLDN data, BPA developed a custom GIS application called the Lightning Strike Analyzer. This application is used in several ways.

First, the lightning data (stored as points) is used to determine whether lightning could have caused an outage. Each point on the map represents a lightning strike and is associated with a database record indicating the date, time, and strength of the strike. Knowing that lightning did not cause an outage is as important as knowing that it did. Secondly, the analyst almost always narrows the search by selecting and buffering a transmission line, and then filtering the data with time, which can be a specific time or a time range. Finally, flash density grids are used to determine whether protective equipment is justified and for planning new transmission line routes.

In the example seen here, an analyst has queried the database of over six million lightning flashes covering the last five years. He constructs a simple query that asks "find the lightning flash, if any, that occurred on July 28, 1995, at 2:04:42 P.M." to see if a particular outage that happened at that time might have been caused by lightning.

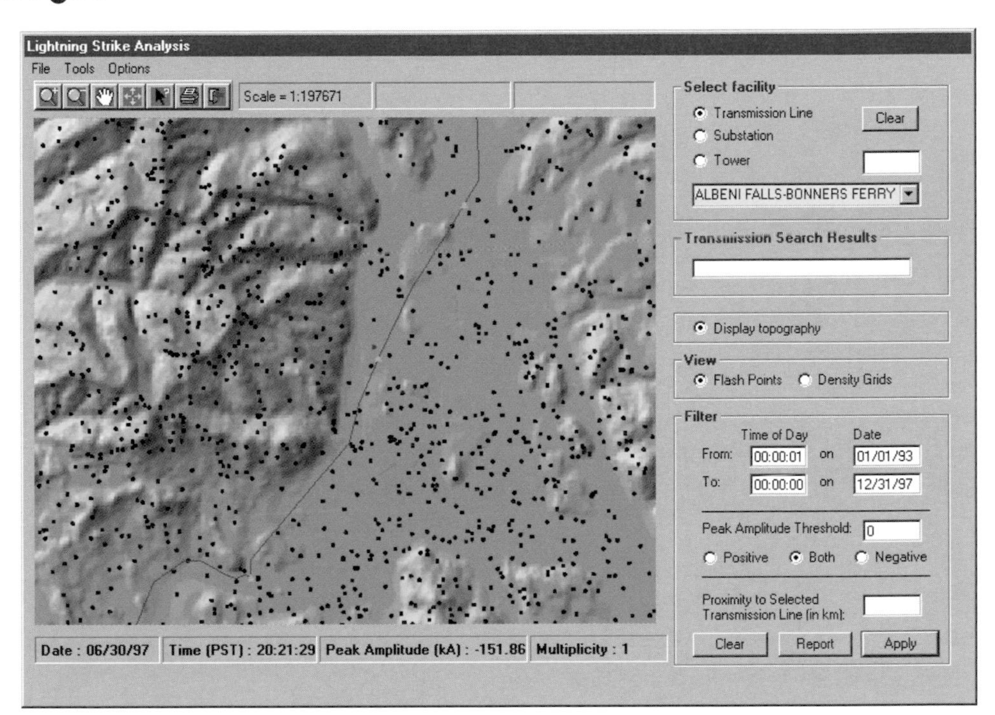

In this example, the user has zoomed in on a transmission line selected from a menu (Albeni Falls-Bonner Ferry). The data for an individual flashpoint (shown in red) is displayed at the bottom of the map.

Advanced flash analysis

The previous example analyzed specific lightning flashes to see if a correlation could be made between power outages and lightning strikes.

But BPA also wants to predict which of its facilities is most likely to be struck by lightning so that protective equipment—equipment too costly to use everywhere—can be installed on just the most vulnerable parts of the system.

In the example on this page, the analyst has entered a buffer of 3 kilometers around the selected transmission line and is looking for flashes that have occurred within the past five days. The cluster of red dots shows that one transmission tower in particular is at greater risk because lightning has struck nearby so many times. This tower is a good candidate for shielding equipment.

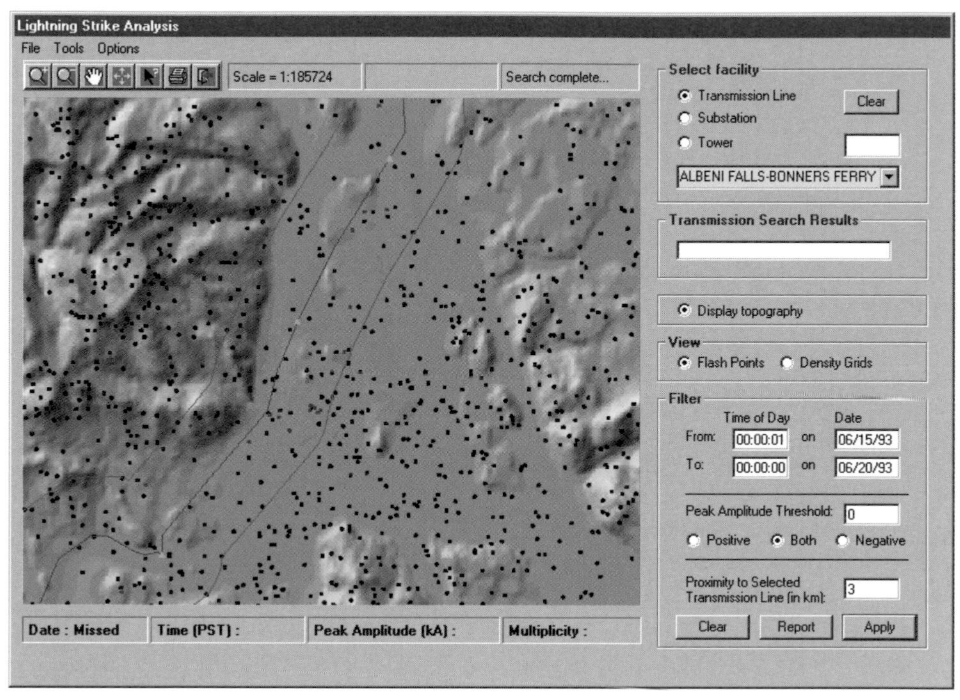

The red dots clustered near the center of the map show all the lightning strikes that occurred during a five-day period in 1993. The tower (shown as a green dot) located just above and to the left of this cluster is likely to be damaged by lightning and should be considered a candidate for protective equipment.

Flash density grids

The application also allows the analyst to summarize all the flash locations by converting the data to something called a flash density grid, which aggregates the individual point data into a series of uniformly sized cells.

The grid representation is useful because it allows the user to generate statistics about the grid that can be compared mathematically to other grids (from different time periods or locations). He can then quickly compare sequential grids that, for example, show the same month over several years to identify problem areas that may be causing outages.

So while the point data is good for visual inspection and interpretation, the grid data is good for more quantitative comparisons.

BPA dispatchers also use lightning data to reroute power if the magnitude and frequency of flashes in an approaching storm warrant it. The use of the archival database and GIS is relatively new. Originally, they did analyses on a "per request" basis. As the frequency of requests grew, they wrote an ARC/INFO client for the requestors to use themselves. With the advent of ARC/INFO software's Open Development Environment (ODE) on Windows NT, they rewrote the application in Microsoft Visual Basic® for the desktop environment.

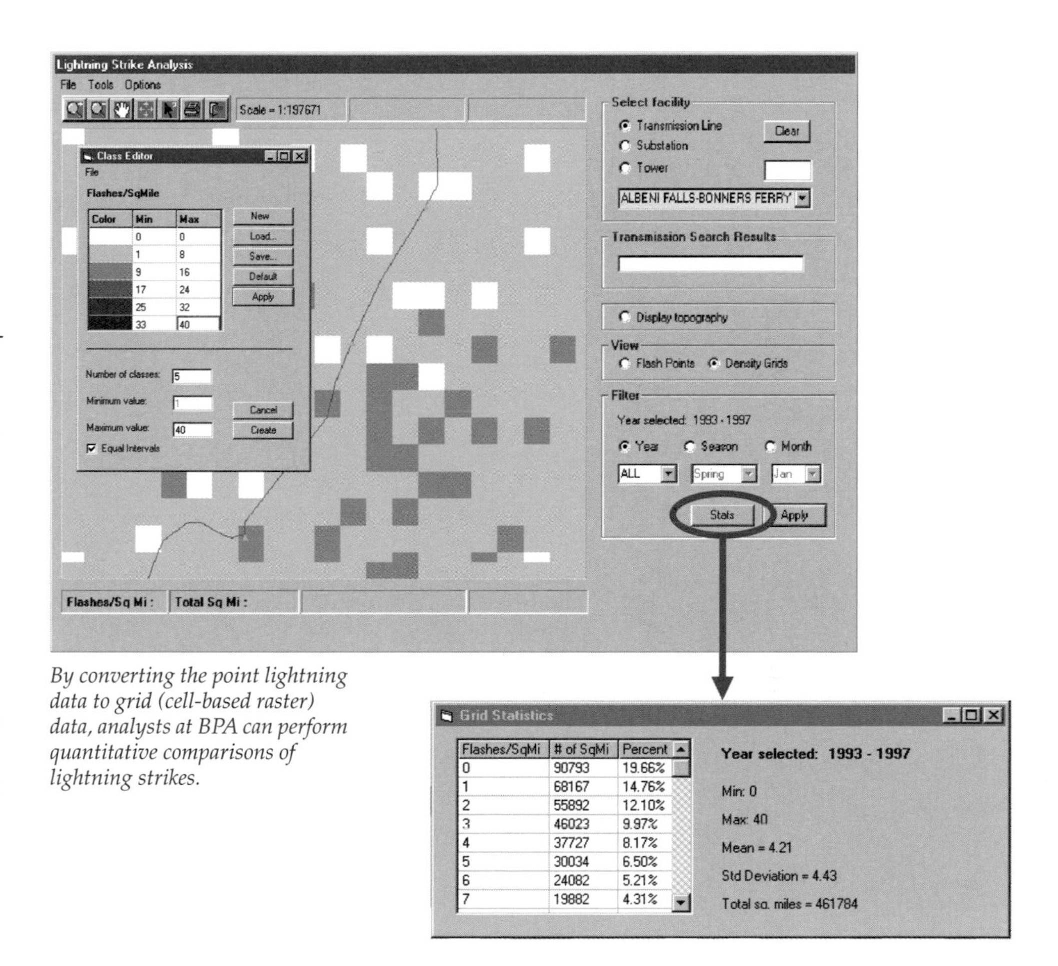

By converting the point lightning data to grid (cell-based raster) data, analysts at BPA can perform quantitative comparisons of lightning strikes.

Conclusion

While no one has done a cost/benefit analysis on the system, its users all agree that it has given them information they didn't have before, information that can help them improve the reliability of the existing system, whether it's being used to site a new substation or to commit to the installation of protective equipment.

The system

The flash location database consists of five years' worth of lightning flash data (approximately six million records) stored in Microsoft SQL Server™ version 6.5 accessed with SDE version 3.02. The data includes information regarding the date and time, strength, polarity, and multiplicity of the flash. The application was written in Microsoft Visual Basic version 5 using ARC/INFO ODE version 7.21 for Windows NT.

Acknowledgments

Thanks to Steve Sherer and Bob White of Bonneville Power Administration.

Bonneville Power Administration

Chapter 8

Automating plan submittals

Planning a residential or commercial real estate development is a complex undertaking. Design plans and drawings must be exchanged between the developer and the local agencies that will provide water, gas, electricity, and other services to the new area. A daunting amount of paperwork is generated.

In this chapter, you'll see how one city in Colorado uses an Internet-based information system to reduce the paperwork and speed up the planning process.

Managing growth

Colorado Springs Utilities is a municipal utility owned by the citizens of Colorado Springs, Colorado, and managed by its city council.

CSU provides the more than 420,000 residents of Colorado Springs and surrounding communities with natural gas, electricity, water, and sewer service. CSU must review every new residential or commercial development project to make sure it meets city codes. It must then decide how best to extend the utilities out to the new homes or businesses.

Job growth and ready land availability have led to a fast-paced development environment in the area. In response, CSU has implemented information technology to help it manage its development overview responsibilities.

In Colorado Springs, new housing developments like this one need power, sewer, gas, and water services.

Getting permits

In order to get building permits, developers must explain precisely what they'll be doing and how they intend to meet the city's strict development codes. This information has historically been presented as paper blueprints depicting master plans, annexation plats, and engineering drawings.

Even for a relatively modest project, such as building a single custom home, a developer would have to make several visits to different city and CSU agencies to drop off and pick up drawings and permits. For larger residential and commercial developments, this phase of a project can be expensive.

When CSU began developing its GIS database in the early nineties, it saw that it could use the technology to reduce the flood of paperwork to the merest trickle. But only in the past few years did the costs of doing so finally make economic sense. By waiting until the hardware and software costs came down, CSU was able to implement a GIS for a fraction of what it would have cost just three years before.

And in an effort to cut the cost of the system quickly, one of the first applications developed was a system for automating the permit review process called DAS, for Development Automation System.

The paper blueprint, while still a mainstay of the construction business, is being replaced in the Colorado Springs permit and design review process by electronic plan submittal.

Submitting plans

A developer in the final stages of designing a retail center to be called the Village at Cottonwood has made some last-minute changes to the plan and must submit the revisions to CSU for approval. She creates a new map reflecting the changes.

In the old days, the next step would have been to print a revised blueprint and deliver it to the CSU offices. But this developer was participating in the DAS project, so she just logged onto the DAS site on the World Wide Web, entered the password and user name, and submitted the drawing electronically as a .dxf file to CSU.

The digital exchange format (DXF) is a standard digital file format in the CAD software programs, such as AutoCAD®, that are widely used by architects and engineers. The ARC/INFO GIS software used by CSU can read .dxf files and also convert them to ARC/INFO coverages or shapefiles for integration into the CSU spatial database.

What used to take at least an hour has been accomplished by the developer in minutes.

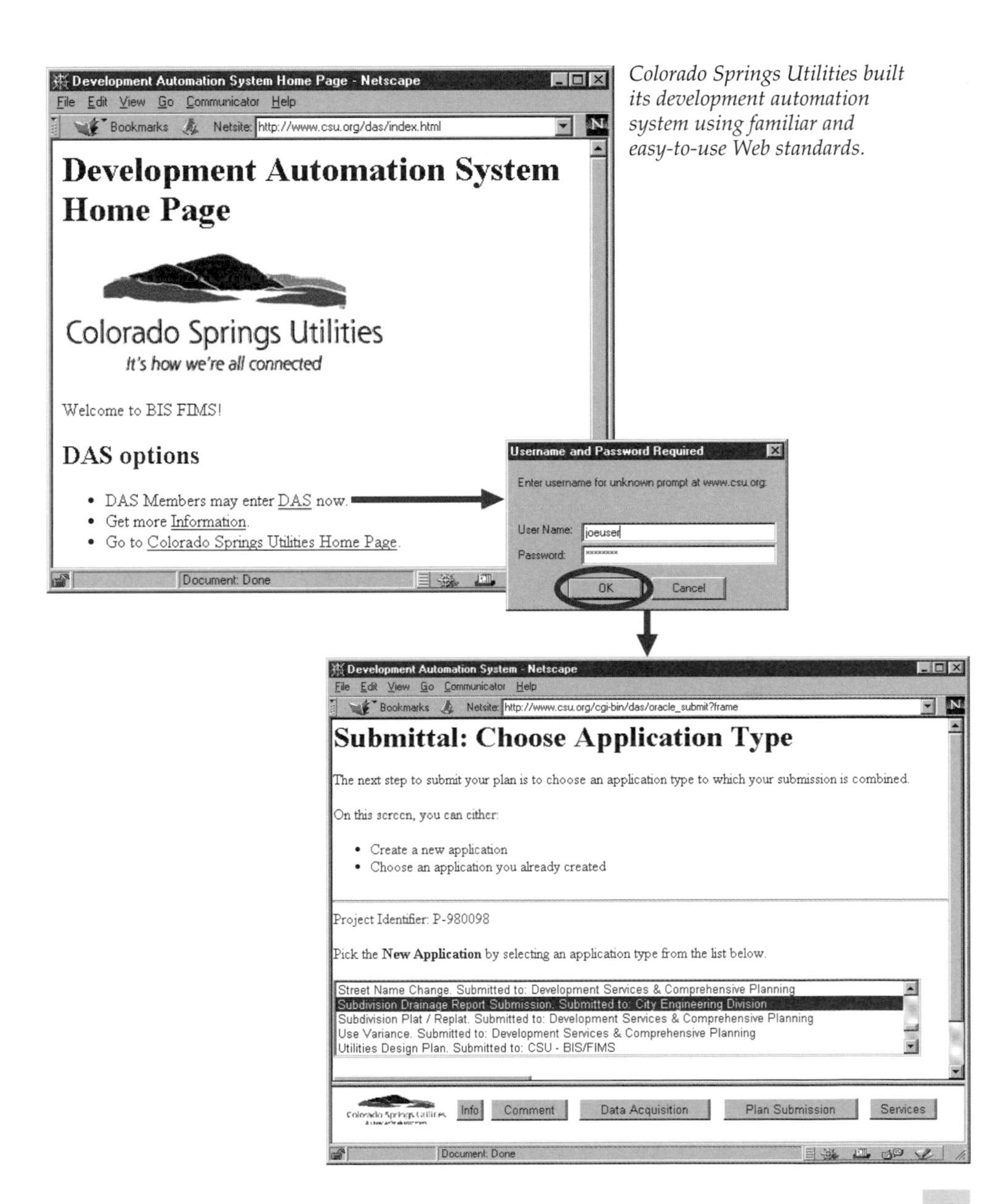

Colorado Springs Utilities built its development automation system using familiar and easy-to-use Web standards.

Beginning the review

Back at CSU offices, an e-mail automatically generated by the system notifies the reviewers that a revised plan for the Village at Cottonwood has been submitted.

Within moments of the plan's having been updated at the developer's crosstown office, it's in the hands of the reviewers and on its way to approval.

Using a custom ArcView GIS application called the DAS Desktop Reviewer, a reviewer pulls up the revised development plan by making the appropriate choices from a series of lists. The reviewer then overlays utility data on the revised plan to see how the changes will affect existing infrastructure.

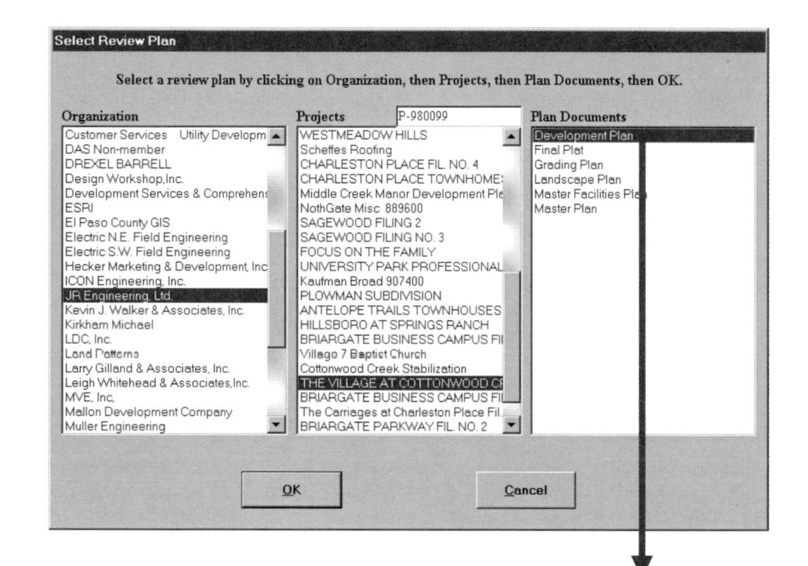

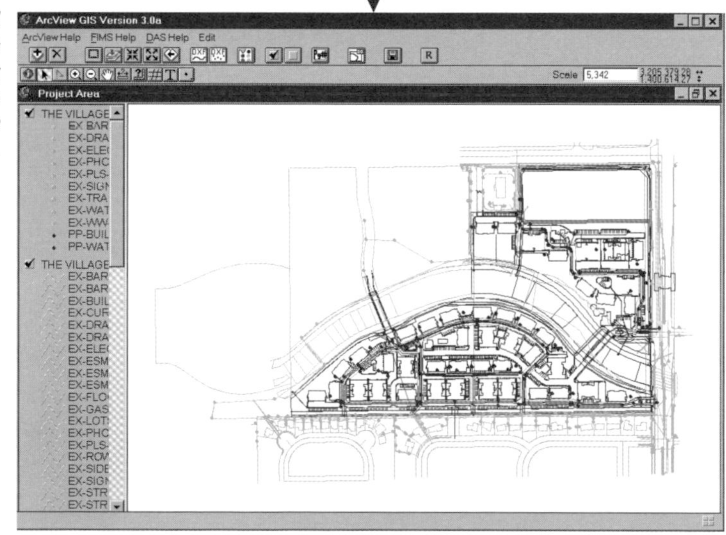

A plan submitted electronically to CSU at 2:17 P.M. on a Friday afternoon is on-screen at the CSU review offices at 2:19.

Adding more data

Once the project drawing is displayed, the reviewer can add utilities layers from the FIMS database by selecting from a list. In this case, he displays layers showing streets, gas and water mains, and electrical underground wires. (FIMS is the name of the CSU database, and is an acronym for Facilities Information Management System.)

Using standard ArcView GIS tools, the reviewer sets the various symbols and colors for each layer to make the map display easier to read.

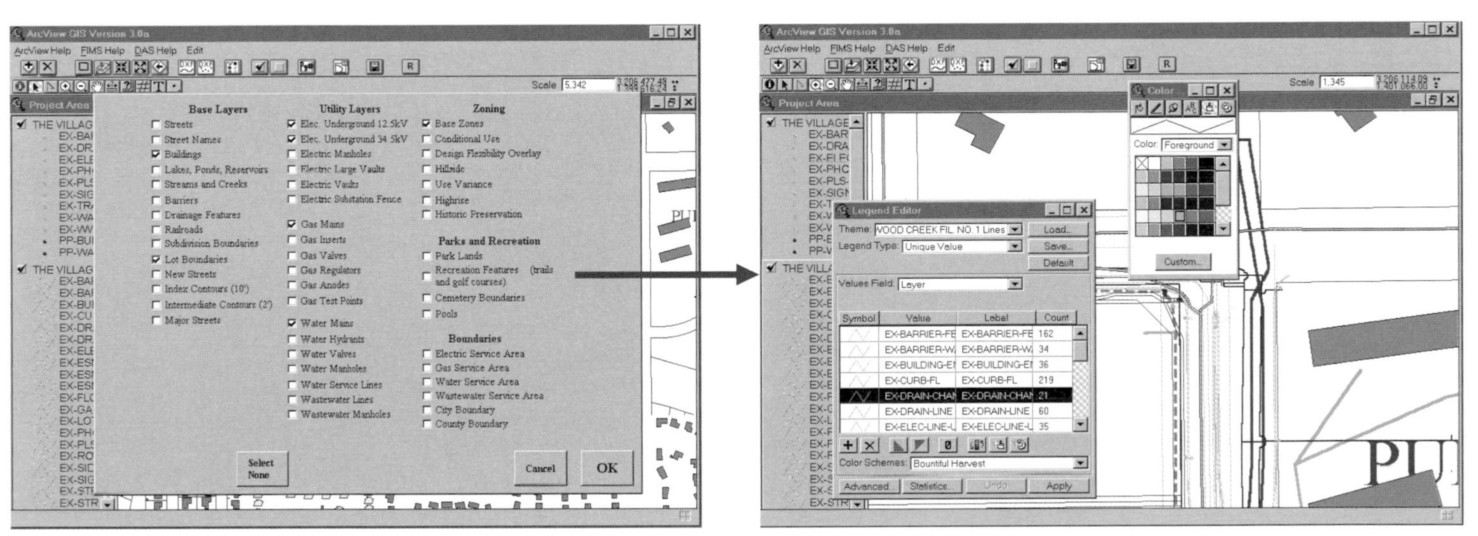

A list of available layers can be turned on or off to facilitate understanding.

Preventing disaster

Using the pan and zoom controls to look at the proposed changes, the reviewer notices that, under the new plan, a section of the as-yet-unbuilt water main has been shifted by about two feet, putting it too close to a sewer line.

The reviewer makes a digital note to this effect on the electronic drawing, saves the information in the database, and e-mails the developer, who can then retrieve the updated file and fix the problem. The review office will not issue the permit until the developer submits a revised plan that meets city building code.

Revisions and reviews are an ordinary part of the development cycle; conducting the business electronically saves the city and the developers tens to hundreds of thousands of dollars annually.

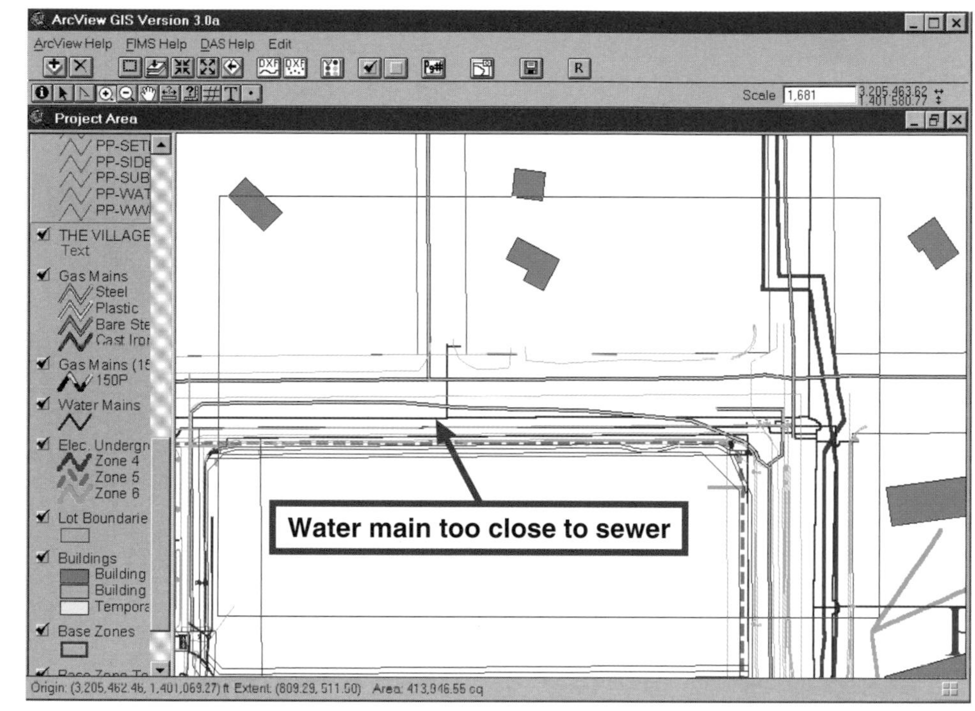

By comparing a digital drawing submitted electronically by a developer with the existing infrastructure stored in the GIS database, a CSU plan reviewer detected a conflict.

System architecture

The system architecture of the DAS is best explained by following a typical DAS session. Users access the Internet from their local PC. They log on to the DAS Web site from the CSU Web server. They begin a data retrieval session on the Web server. A CGI program talks to the Oracle server via a secure firewall. Once the appropriate information has been retrieved from the Oracle server, a GIS data request is delivered to FIMS staff via e-mail through the firewall.

Programs are executed through password-encrypted e-mail messages sent to batch queues that parse the message for program syntax and parameters. When a request is completed, the data is stored on the GIS server for transfer to the Web server and further transfer to the user's PC.

As plan files are submitted, one copy is delivered to the GIS server and another copy goes to an archive host, which writes the files to a compact disc writer. In the event that a submittal is altered down the review path, an original version is available for purposes of comparison.

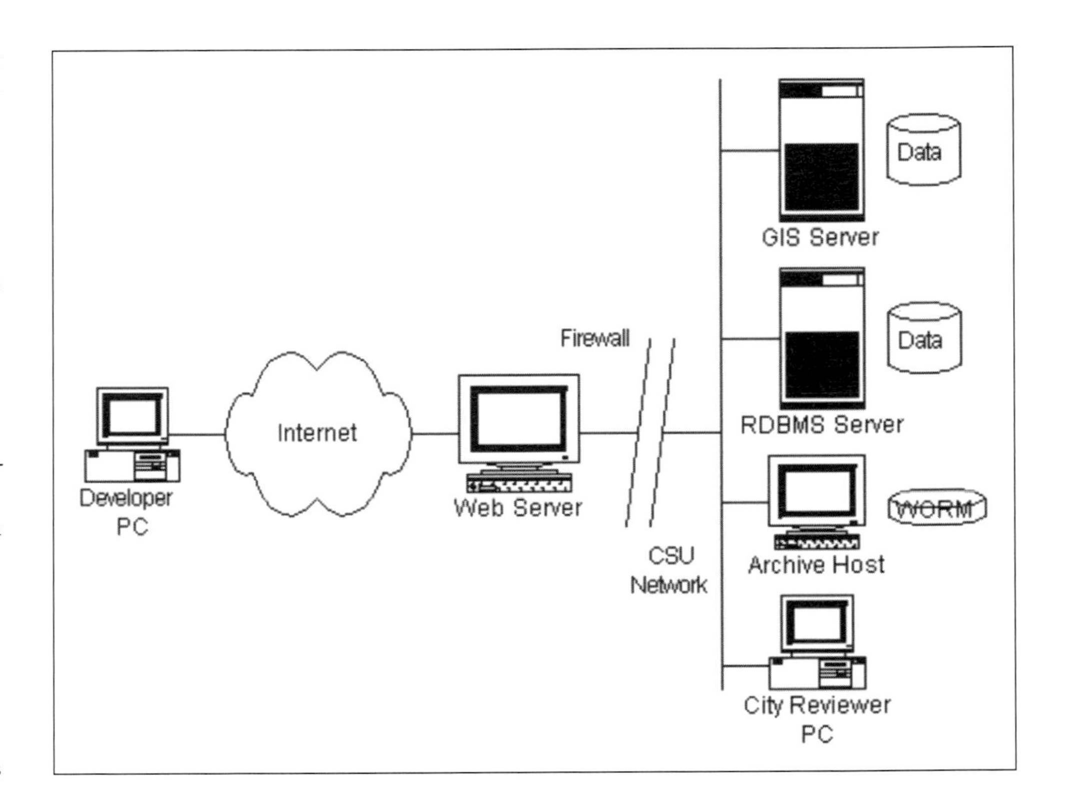

Conclusion

The FIMS staff realized early on that keeping the base mapping up to date in the face of rapid development would represent a considerable expense. At the same time, they recognized that the land development community could be a key source of digital feature data that would keep the FIMS database current. Because this data is available to the development community and the public at large, everyone had something at stake.

The DAS system creates an environment where everyone benefits. By adhering to the data quality specifications set forth by CSU, developers can have their submittals processed and reviewed quickly. The developers benefit from not having to submit the endless rolls of paper drawings that traditionally make up a submittal package. The reviewers can see the project electronically with existing infrastructure displayed in the background, giving them a more thorough understanding of the issues that relate to that project. The overall result is a more streamlined design process that saves money on both sides of the fence.

Acknowledgments

Thanks to James W. Ross and Larry Von De Bur of Colorado Springs Utilities, and to David Totman of Berger & Company.

Colorado Springs Utilities

Chapter 9

Managing transmission lines

We've all seen them along the roads: those miles and miles of wire strung between massive steel and wood structures. They are the high-voltage transmission lines that deliver electricity from power-generating plants to local distribution centers. While we may not give them much thought, without them, not only would our homes be dark, but our entire information-based economy could not function.

In this chapter, you'll see how a public utility in New Mexico uses GIS to tread lightly on the fragile lands across which their transmission lines extend.

Energy for the Southwest

Public Service Company of New Mexico (PNM) is the largest public utility in the state. Serving both gas and electricity to more than one million New Mexicans, the organization employs over twenty-eight hundred people.

The Transmission Engineering Department of PNM Electric Services constructs, operates, and maintains almost 3,000 miles of high-voltage power transmission lines, mainly in rural areas of New Mexico.

On occasion, PNM has inadvertently damaged fragile archaeological sites when service crews had to trail blaze access to remote towers. In an attempt to eliminate these incidents, PNM decided to implement a custom GIS solution that gives service crews all the information they need to find the best way to any PNM tower.

High-voltage transmission lines are the lifelines of modern civilization. Maintaining and repairing these systems create specialized information needs that are ideally met by a GIS.

Introducing TAMIS

Recently, PNM experienced two major events that highlighted the need for the development of a systemwide GIS. The first involved a major power outage. A PNM high-voltage transmission line serving a portion of New Mexico failed. This line traversed a rugged mountainous region, which made it very difficult to gain access to the faulty equipment. With no backup for this particular line, PNM was forced, at great expense, to activate local power-generating systems for an extended period of time to prevent additional outages on the system.

The second incident resulted from normal maintenance and construction work. Crews needed to get to a tower that had no access road. (Years had passed since anyone had been there in a vehicle and the dirt track made during construction had been long since reclaimed by the desert.) PNM crews were forced to bulldoze a road to the structure in order to perform the needed work. Without current and complete information, they disrupted an archaeological site.

Had the crews possessed vital information about access routes, land ownership, and areas to avoid, this accident could have been prevented. Thus, the Transmission Asset Management Information System (TAMIS) was born.

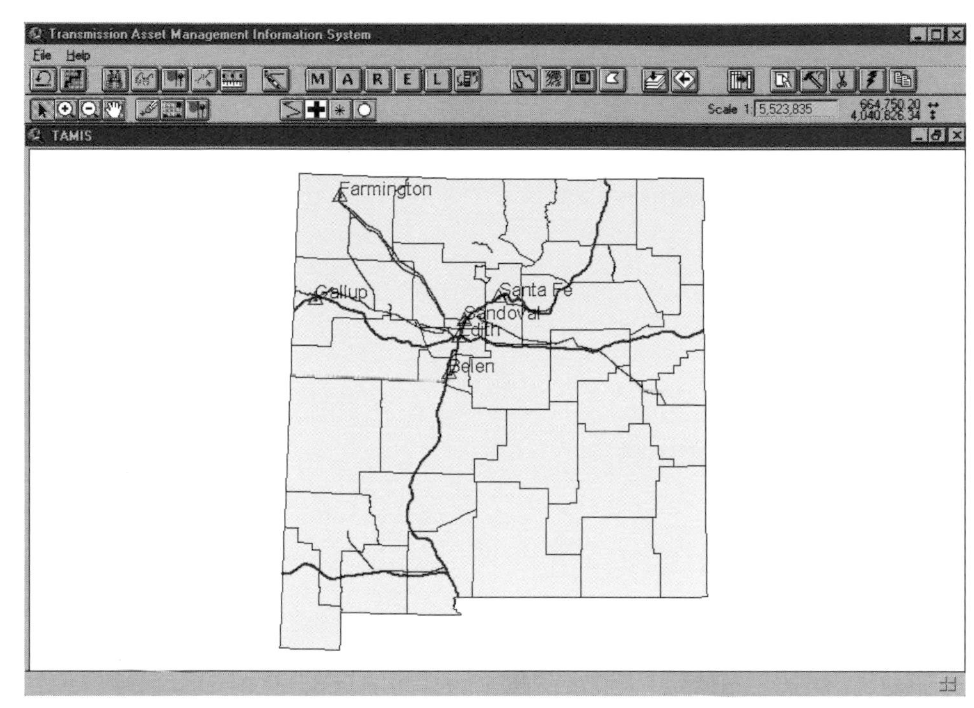

The Transmission Asset Management Information System (TAMIS) was created to provide access information during an emergency. It has earned its keep as a day-to-day management workhorse.

Finding the best route

In the course of using the application, a crew performs two primary operations: finding the best route to a tower or facility, and getting information about that asset.

When the users invoke the route tool, they pick the type of facility they're traveling to. In the case shown, a pole was chosen. Next, they must pick a starting point—a PNM station or communication facility—from a drop-down list of all PNM locations. A dialog box then prompts them to enter a specific pole or tower.

The resulting overview map highlights the best route in pink. Rules built into the routing program ensure that the route will be the most direct path that uses any available known road and does not violate restricted or sensitive lands, even if it goes cross-country where there are no paved roads.

The application also creates a set of turn-by-turn directions that can be printed out and that include an exact mileage calculation.

But use of TAMIS does not end at the office: crews also have the application loaded on their laptop computers. As you'll see, this allows them to orient themselves as they approach the site.

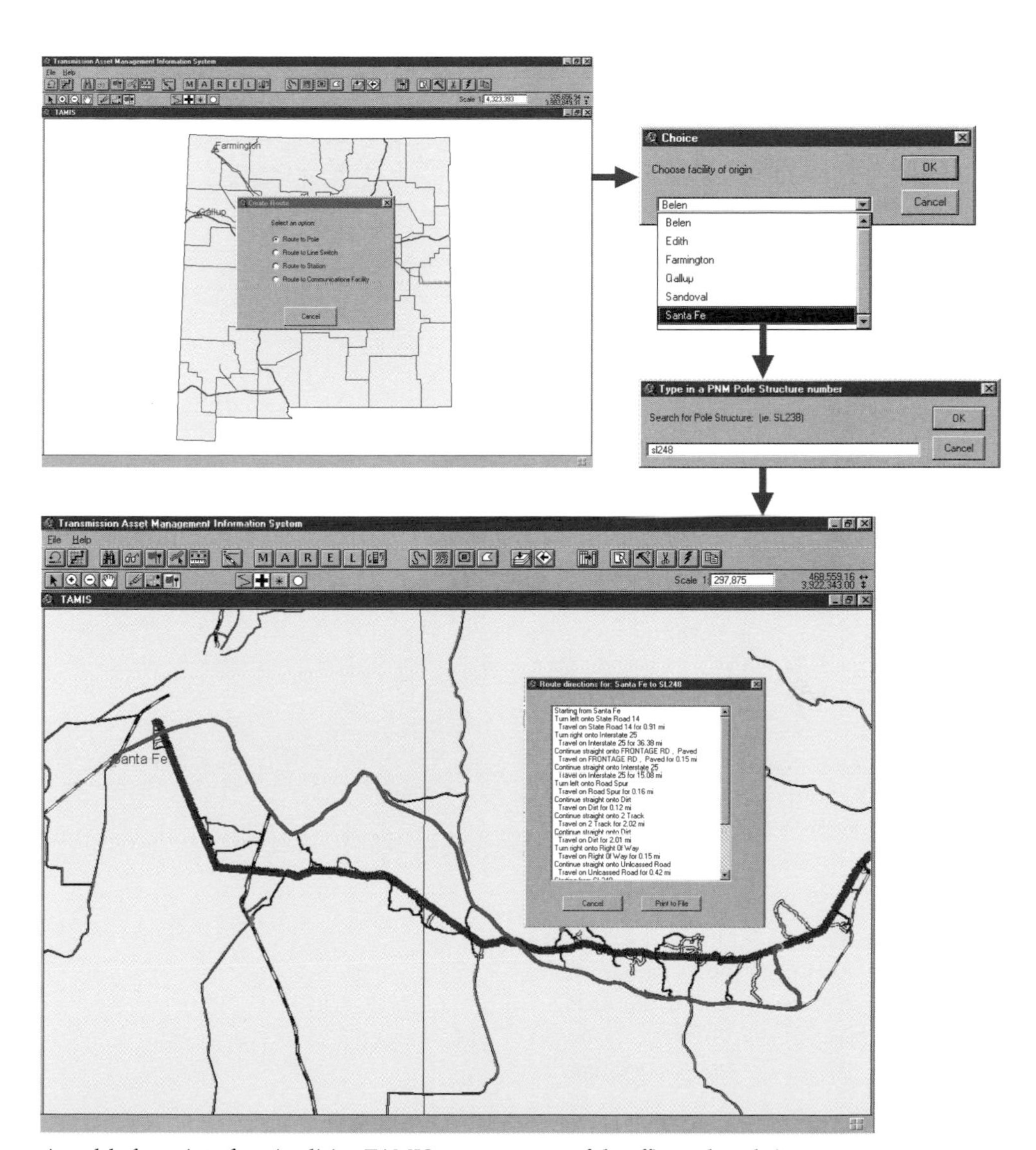

A model of user interface simplicity, TAMIS gets crews out of the office and on their way to the job site in seconds.

As the truck approaches the pole or structure to be serviced, the crew boss can zoom in on the map to reveal more detail. Topographical maps appear underneath the route information. The crew can also refer to the legend on the left of the screen to see what grade of road they'll encounter as they travel. Another tool incorporated in the program allows the crew to view, on-screen, live GPS tracking to ensure the correct route is followed.

At this scale, they can begin to see individual poles on the map. In this case, they have used another feature of the system to display all the poles colored according to the current maintenance classification. (PNM classifies needed maintenance required on a scale of 1 to 4 as follows: 1—Critical; 2—Medium; 3—Low; and 4—None.)

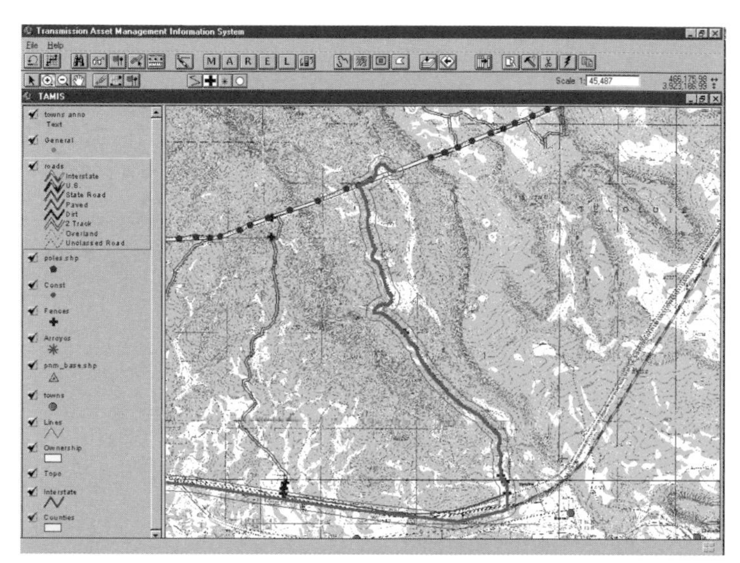

This screen shows the correct and safe approach to the destination structure, as well as to other structures in the area. The topographical map in the background aids in orienting the crews to the surrounding landscape.

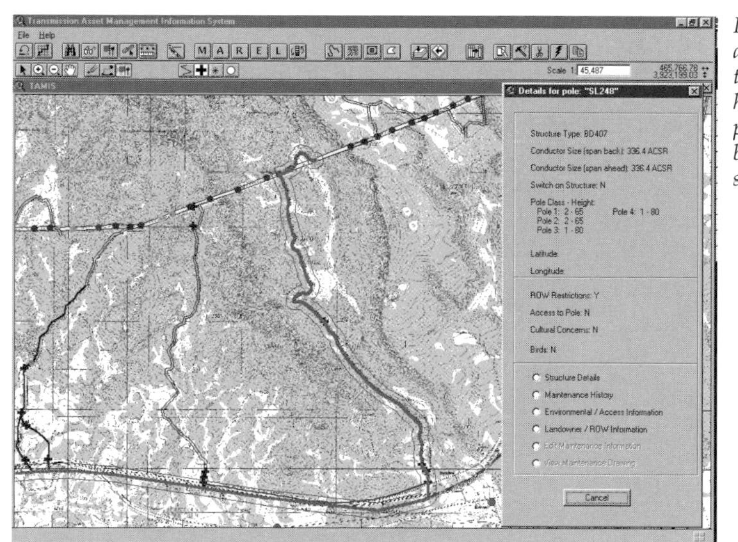

In this view, the poles are classified according to their maintenance history and a screen of pole-specific data has been pulled up with a single mouse click.

Working at the site

Once the crew has arrived at the site, the boss begins to access more detailed information—equipment lists, schematic drawings, work history logs. After inspecting a CAD drawing of the entire structure, the boss clicks on a specific component to view a schematic drawing of that component. She also displays a report that gives her the pole's specifications and maintenance history.

As her crew performs its inspections and repairs, she fills out electronic maintenance forms that will allow the updated information to be added to the core database when they return to the office. Many of these structures are so remote that it may have been months or years since they were last inspected. So whenever a crew is sent to any PNM structure, as much information as possible is collected.

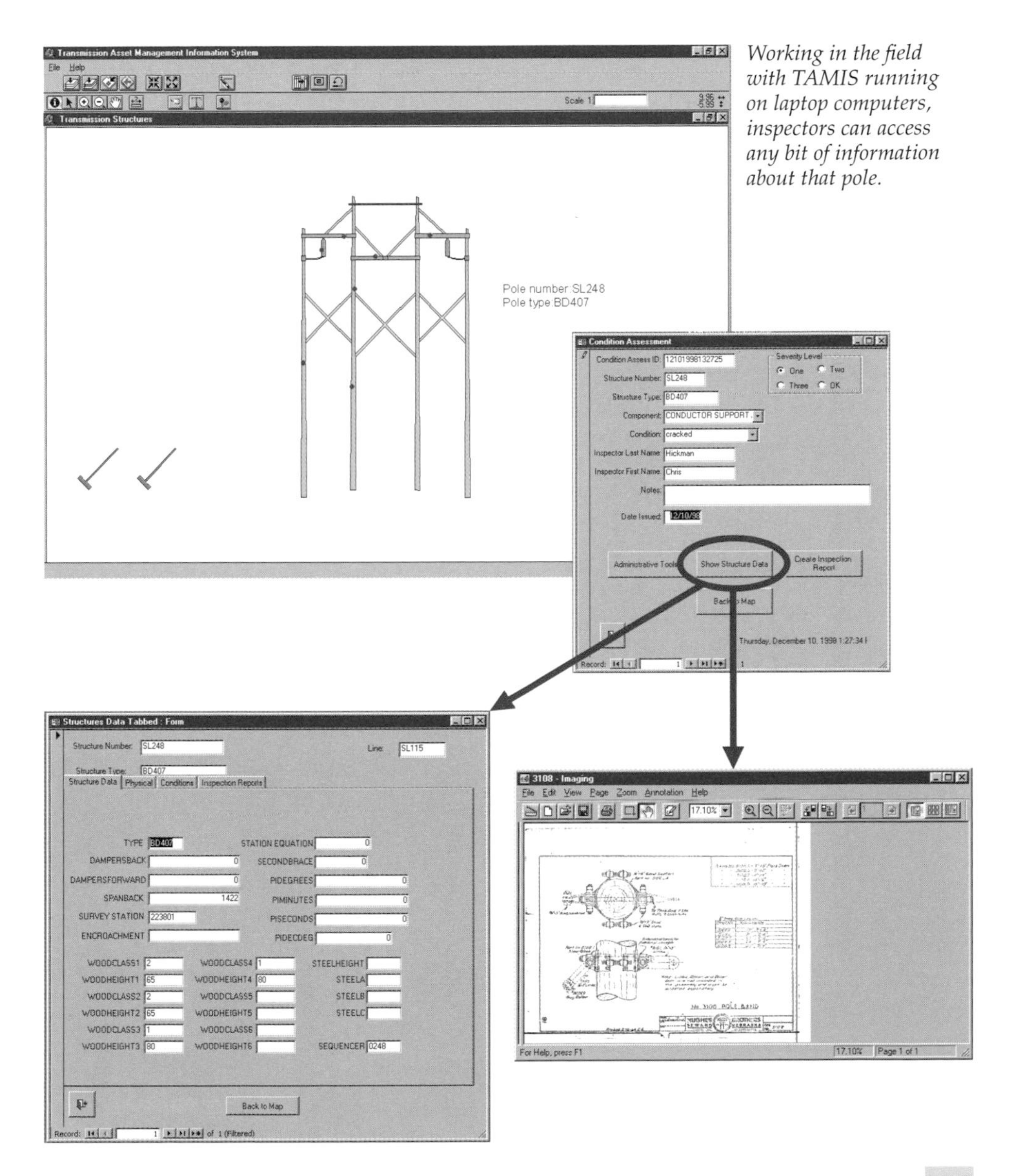

Working in the field with TAMIS running on laptop computers, inspectors can access any bit of information about that pole.

Reports and work orders

Before leaving the site, the inspector must report details about the problem, the equipment required to fix it, how much time was spent, and general notes about the condition of the approach road and the structure itself. All of this will be loaded into the main database at headquarters and will help the next crew that comes the same way.

If the crew discovers damage that's beyond its ability to fix or that requires a replacement part it didn't bring, the boss creates a work order detailing what's needed.

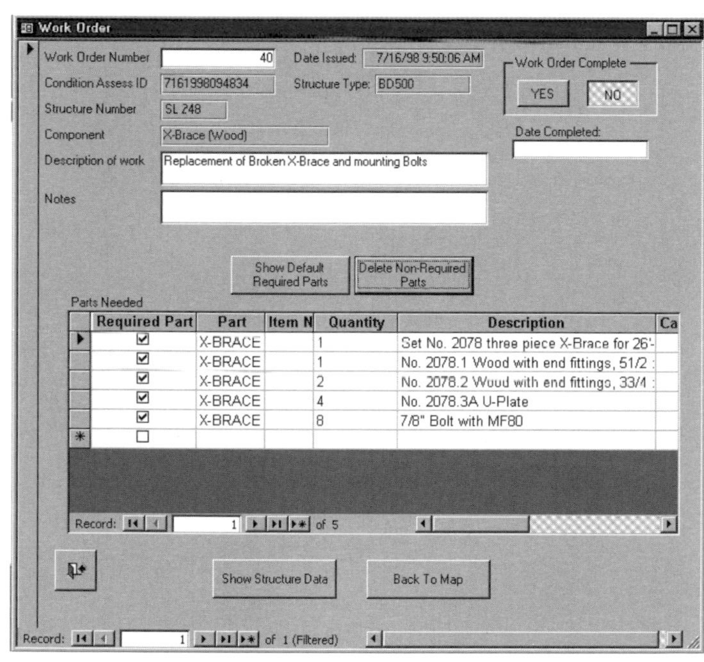

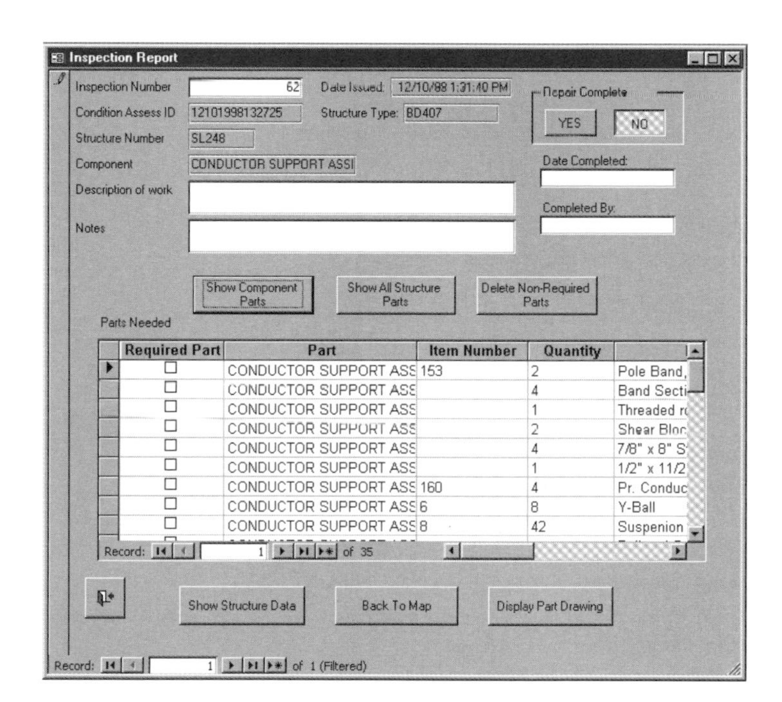

Creating reports and work orders used to be the bane of the field inspector. But with TAMIS it's easy to do.

Conclusion

Since implementing TAMIS, PNM has been able to avoid disturbing sensitive lands. TAMIS also allows PNM to work closely with state and federal agencies as well as Native American governments to identify fragile environmental or historical areas and religious sites and to ensure there are no further environmental or archaeological infractions. The general feeling, from top management to field crews, is that TAMIS allows the company to operate in an efficient, timely, and competitive manner.

Hardware

Laptop Pentium computers

Software

ArcView GIS for Windows

ArcView Network Analyst

Microsoft Access

Acknowledgments

Thanks to Ted Hircher and Chris Hickman of Public Service Company of New Mexico.

Chapter 10

Gas across America

Unless you happen to live in Alaska or Texas, the gas for your stove and water heater and furnace comes from much farther away than the pipes under your house. It's conveyed from its production sites through miles of huge, high-capacity gas pipelines.

In this chapter, you'll see how the nation's largest transporter of compressed natural gas uses GIS technology to make information about its pipelines available from a digital map.

Managing linear assets

Williams Gas Pipeline, a corporation made up of five pipeline subsidiaries, transports more compressed natural gas to American homes and industry than anyone else.

Until recently, the five pipeline companies operated independently. But competitive pressure and regulatory constraints eventually made it sensible for them to merge.

After banding together under the Williams umbrella, the corporate managers' first step was to consolidate and reengineer their information system. Due to the fact that these pipelines must pass over all sorts of public and private property, the only kind of information system that made sense was one based on geography.

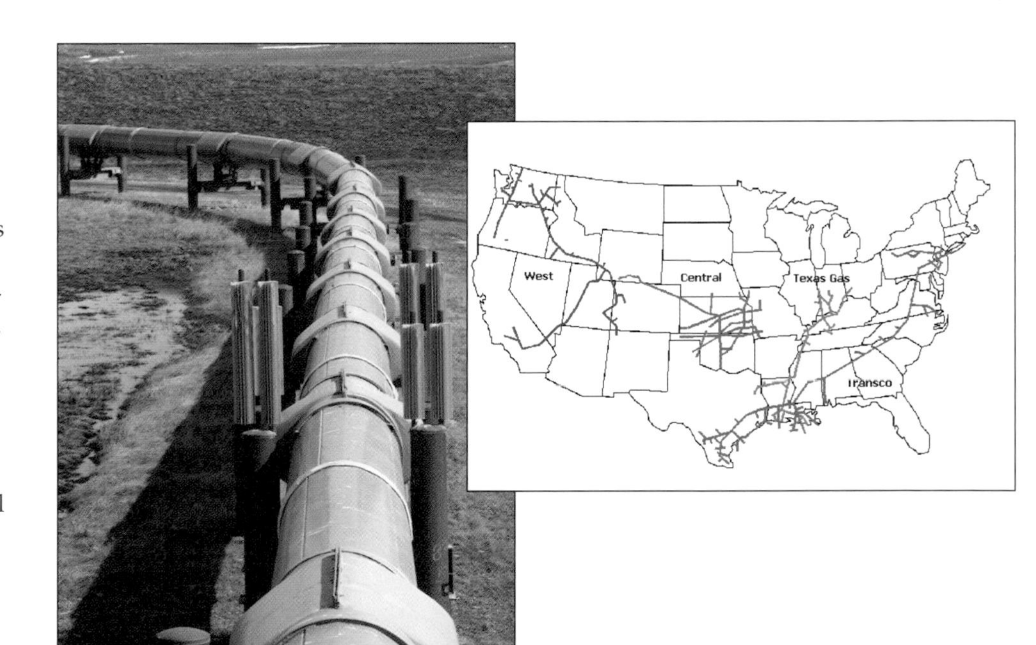

Mile after mile, pipelines like this one carry natural gas to your home. The Williams Gas Pipeline network spans the country.

The pipeline model

The digital pipeline model created for the GIS is really two models: the first is the representation of pipes, valves, and stations that make up the physical pipeline along with information about them: pipe diameter, operating pressure, and how soon until maintenance. This data is represented in the spatial database as line segments.

The second model is the representation of the land that the pipe traverses. This land ownership record contains all the information about the permissions and contracts that allow the pipeline to cross over public and private property. This information is stored in the database as polygons.

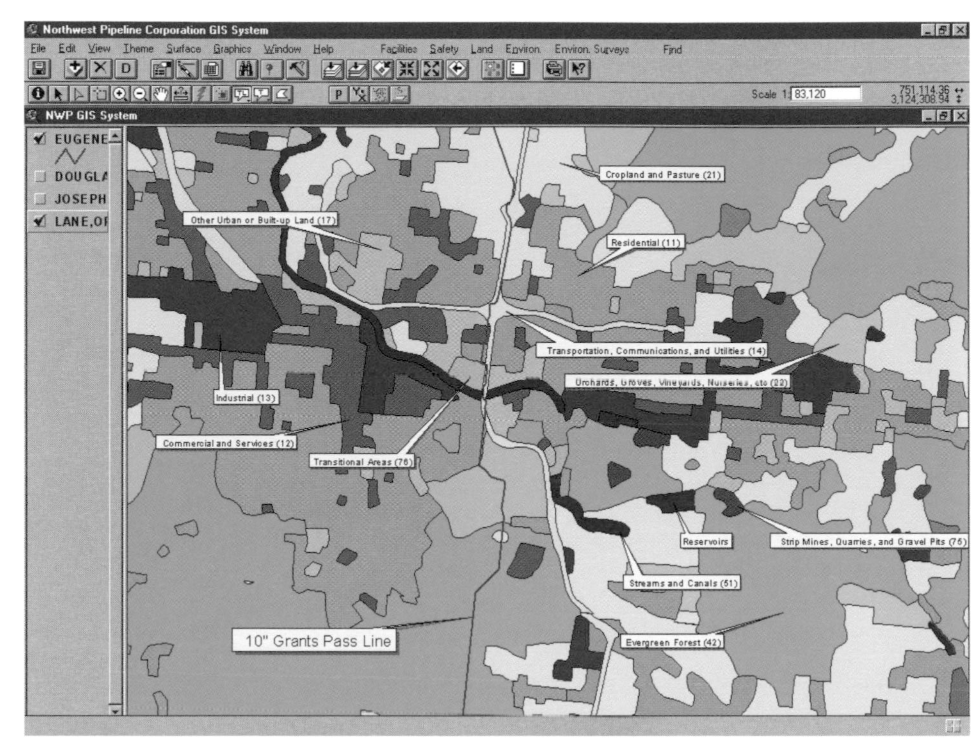

This map shows the variety of land uses that the pipelines of WGP must cross over to move natural gas through Grant's Pass, Oregon. Each time the pipeline crosses into different land usage, it means that WGP has some sort of agreement with the landowner. Keeping track of these relationships in their GIS is the job of the pipeline managers.

How the two models interact

From their origins at the processing facilities to their destinations at local distribution centers, the company's pipelines cross thousands of boundaries and lines. These may be ownership or political boundaries (where a piece of private property begins and ends, where a national forest starts) or they may be physical features like power cables. Every time one of these lines is crossed, all available information about it must be saved in a database.

Another way of looking at the database is to follow the pipeline in the electronic model and use the identify tool to select each feature that it crosses. In the case of the pipeline crossing a piece of private property as seen at the right, this would bring up information about the property including its size, what structures are built on it, and who owns it.

Having all the information in one database makes the day-to-day operation of the business more efficient because managers can spend their time dealing with real problems and issues, not chasing down information from myriad paper and electronic sources.

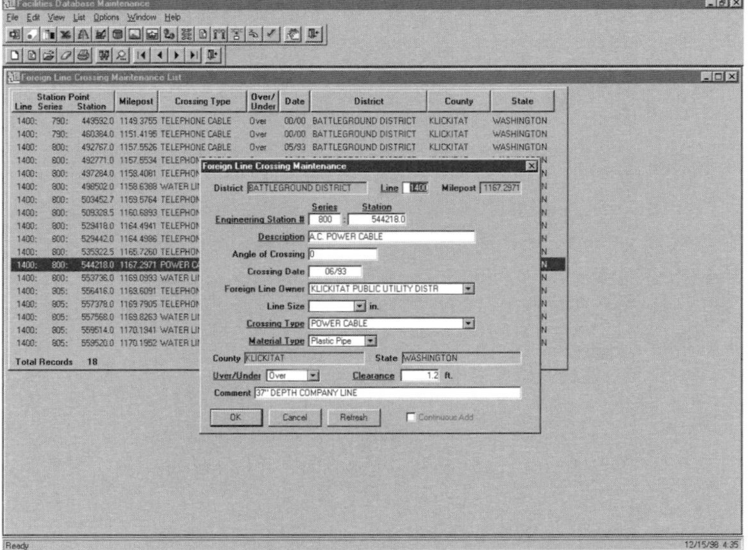

The record shows that at mile 1,167, the 10-inch Grants Pass pipeline crosses a Klickitat Public Utility District AC Power Cable. The gas pipeline is 37 inches deep; the cable is 1.2 feet over the pipeline.

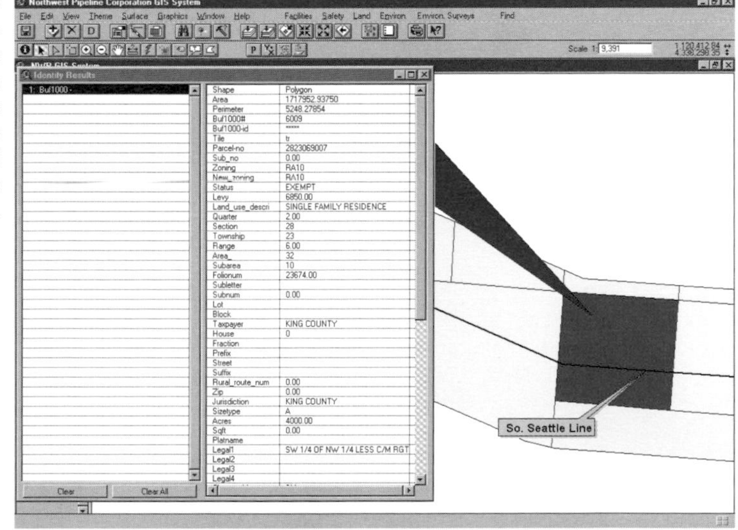

Here we see a parcel of private property being crossed. We can see the dimensions (4,000 acres), the type of zoning (single family residence), and the tax status (exempt).

Alignment sheet

An interesting and useful document (originally devised by pipeline mapping pioneers) is something called an alignment sheet. Alignment sheets combine schematic drawings registered to photographic images with database records.

Alignment sheets include an extraordinary amount of information. Because they are detailed and large-scale, it can take thousands of alignment sheets to depict the full length of a pipeline. Producing them used to require both drafting skills and familiarity with a number of rather esoteric software packages. Today, these documents can be generated on demand and output in minutes as opposed to the hundreds of hours they used to take.

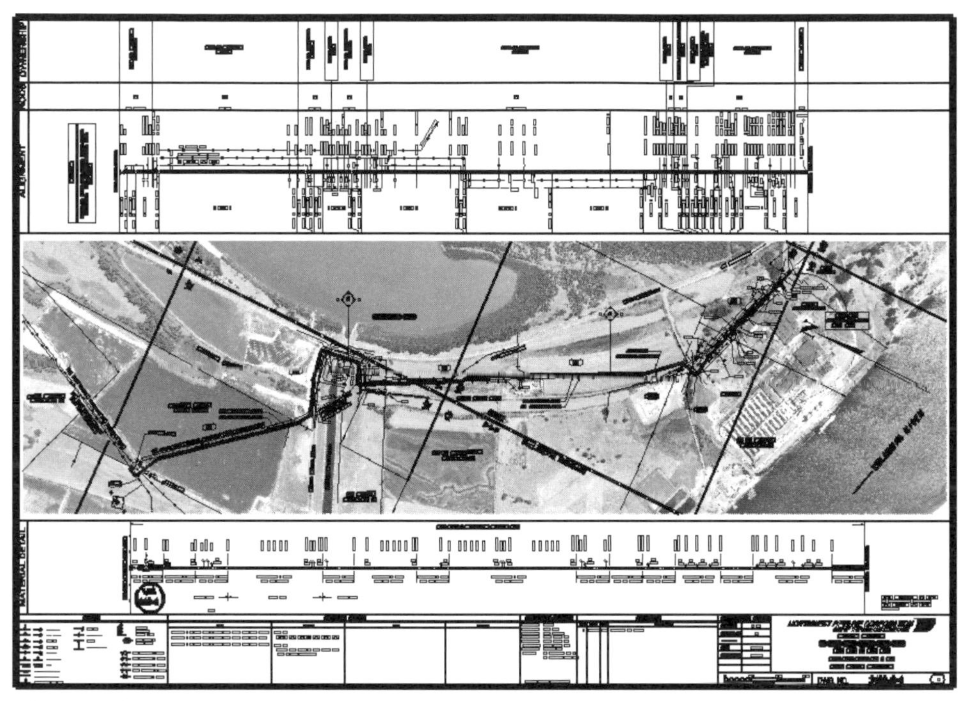

Alignment sheets get their name from the fact that schematic drawings of pipelines (which have no real-world location information) are matched up, or aligned, with georeferenced images of the terrain.

Mitigating environmental impact

As open space dwindles, the public agencies and private organizations that manage it are under increasing pressure to make sure that what's left as open space is preserved and protected.

But a gas pipeline must often pass through environmentally sensitive lands if it is to fulfill its purpose. This is part of the trade-off we make by demanding natural gas to heat our homes and cook our meals. Legislation and public opinion make it crucial that WGP not pollute or damage the landscape.

WGP recently assessed its operations in an area east of Bellingham, Washington, where a section of pipeline crosses the Nooksack River. The company wanted to see if the pipeline was driving birds from their nesting grounds.

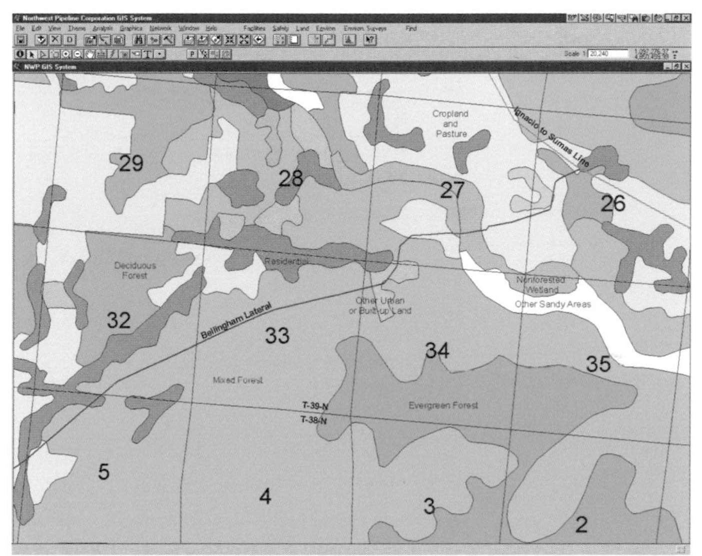

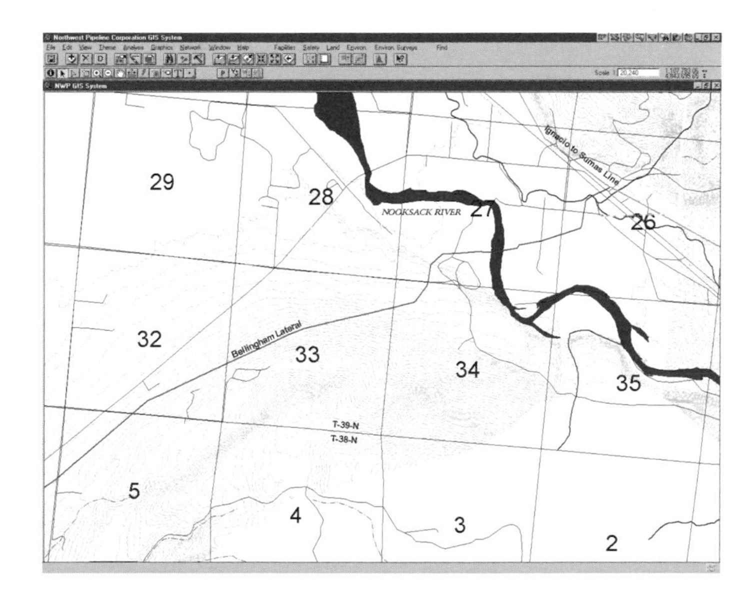

The Nooksack River in Washington State is a place where migrating birds, many of them endangered, come to nest. These maps show different views (one according to land use, the other by land form) of how the company's Bellingham Lateral Pipeline traverses this environmentally sensitive area.

Studying bird nesting patterns

The analysis showed that most species continued to nest close to the pipeline, apparently undisturbed by its presence.

The system also allowed staff members working on regulatory compliance to be equipped with clear and accurate presentations of the situation. Data displayed in the context of geography is easy for audiences to understand and enables the organization to make its case in a cogent and persuasive manner.

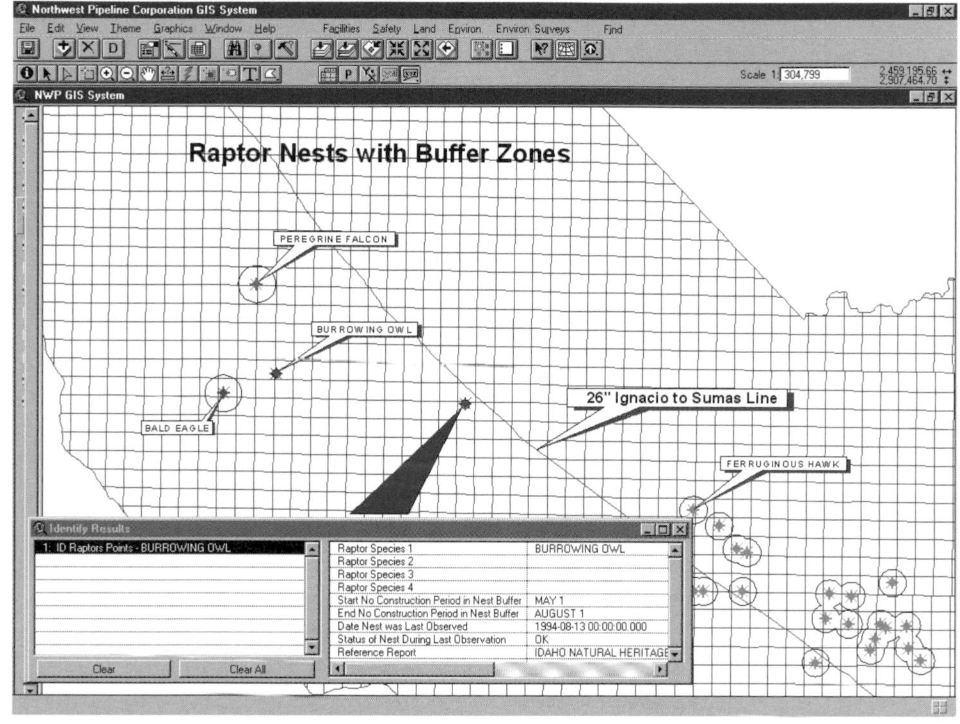

Using data collected in the field by government biologists, environmental managers at WGP can see exactly how well they're doing.

Conclusion

In 1999, the company will have a fully implemented GIS for all of Williams Gas Pipeline, including WGP–Transco, WGP–Texas Gas, WGP–Central, and WGP–West. The GIS will include over 28,000 miles of the pipeline system from coast to coast. The GIS will be common to all pipelines and have fully developed GIS applications.

Hardware

PC-compatible laptop and desktop computers

Software

ArcView GIS for Windows

ArcView Network Analyst

Microsoft Access

ARC/INFO

Sybase®

Acknowledgments

Thanks to Leon Ruflin and Julie Zwemke of Williams Gas Pipeline, Salt Lake City, Utah.

Chapter 11

Service technician routing

For organizations that employ legions of mobile service technicians, using computers to automate the complex sequencing of their routes can boost productivity tremendously. For large operations, the difference between a poorly planned route and a well-planned one can be measured in millions of dollars (not to mention greatly improved customer satisfaction). GIS analysis of transportation networks coupled with intranet access to the information has allowed many service organizations to fully realize those benefits.

In this chapter, you'll see an application developed for a large gas utility to automate routes for its service technicians, and you'll see how putting the system on the company intranet will greatly improve its routing operations.

Glad to be of service℠

Southern California Gas Company (Los Angeles, California) is the largest distributor of natural gas in the United States, serving over seventeen million people through some 45,000 miles of distribution and transmission pipelines.

Unlike telephone or electric service, which can be switched on and off from a central location, the nature of gas service dictates that technicians must go where it's being delivered. Over one thousand of the company's more than seven thousand employees work as customer service technicians.

For this reason, managers use the latest information technology (like GIS and the Internet) to do the best job possible in keeping the field work organized.

Southern California Gas Company uses advanced information technology including handheld computers and GIS to route field service technicians more efficiently.

Where it all starts

The standard way for customers to request service is to telephone SoCalGas. To better serve its busy (and increasingly Internet-connected) customers, the company recently added a new way to schedule a service visit: the World Wide Web. By logging onto the SoCalGas Web site at www.socalgas.com, customers can now submit their requests online, at any time of day or night.

SoCalGas receives thousands of requests for service each day: requests to have the gas turned on when someone moves into a new home or business or turned off when someone moves out, requests for gas appliance repairs and adjustments, and even requests to have pilots lit.

SoCalGas operates fifty-two service facilities in five regions. Each of these facilities employs anywhere from twenty to fifty service technicians, and each technician handles between twenty and sixty service calls per day. With this many people on the road, the company wants its routes to be as efficient as possible.

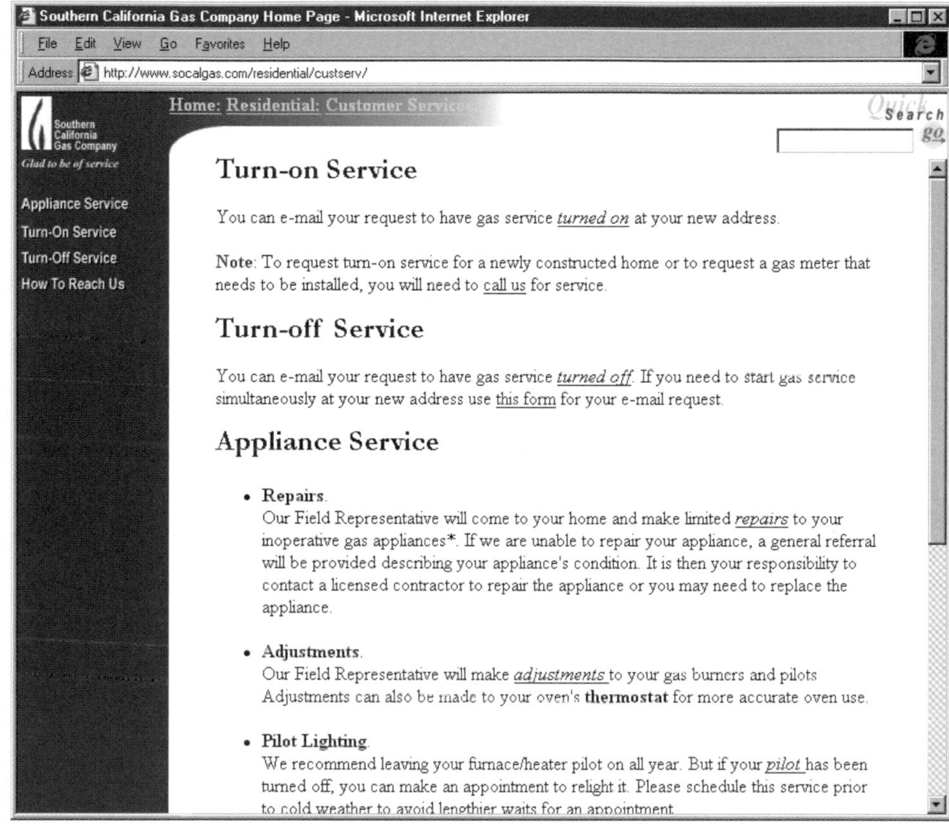

You can go to the SoCalGas Web site to ask that your gas be turned on or off.

The magic of automated routing

The service requests are stored as database records in a mainframe information system called PACER. SoCalGas employees known as routers group these service orders into routes and download them to the Geographic Routing and Integrated Dispatch (GRID) system. Each service order includes the type of job, the address of the home or business requiring service, and the estimated amount of time required to do the work.

A computer model of streets covering the company's entire service area is stored in the GRID system. Using ESRI's NetEngine™ technology, the GRID application considers all the stops on each technician's route and arranges them in the best visiting order. Sophisticated software algorithms take into account everything about the street network that will affect the route planning, like one-way streets and speed limits.

Once all the stops that have been assigned to a technician are sequenced, the service orders are downloaded to handheld computers for the next day, and also converted to shapefile paths. These are automatically loaded into an ArcView Internet Map Server application for serving over the company's internal network, or intranet.

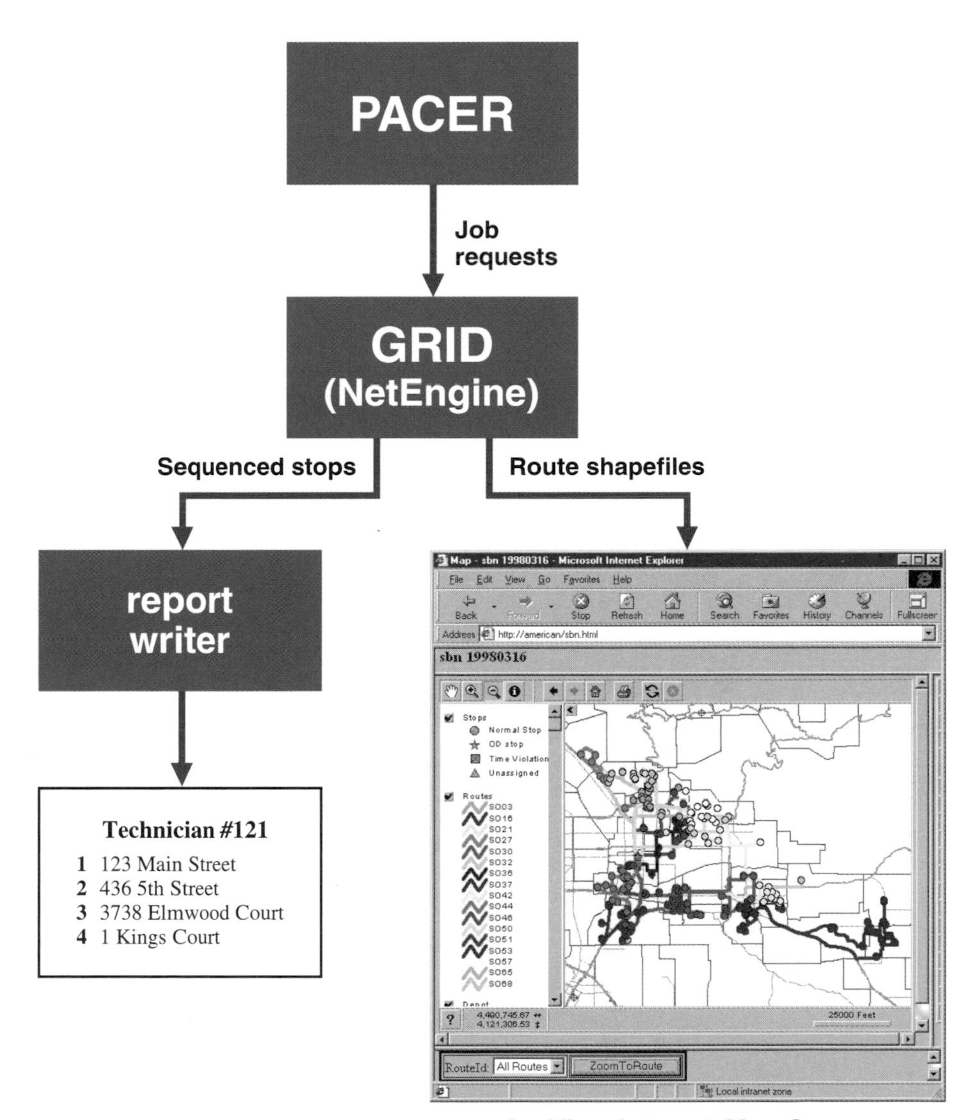

ArcView Internet Map Server

The map interface

The finished routes for each service technician can be displayed as different-colored paths on a street map.

Once the route maps have been put online via the intranet, the routers will be able to check the work in their Web browsers to make sure it makes logical sense. If anything seems amiss, the router can change it and reload the Web page to see the update. In fact, the ability to get to the route information using only a Web browser and no additional GIS software will make it much easier for all levels of SoCalGas administration to understand the routing function.

For each service facility, the default view is zoomed out to an extent wide enough to include all the routes. The tools across the top of the map allow users to zoom in on specific areas, pan the map, and query the data behind the routes.

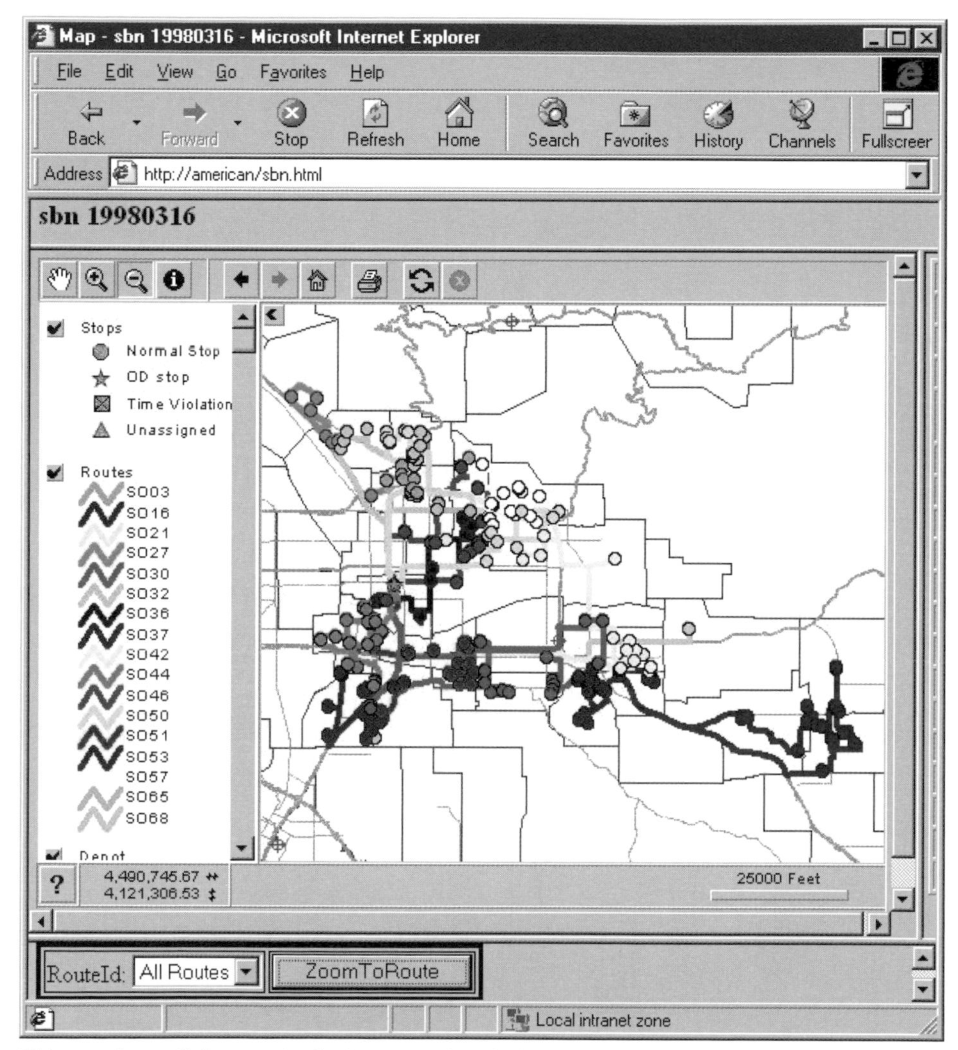

This map shows all the stops for the San Bernardino facility, assigned to more than seventeen routes.

Looking at a single route

Using the popup list at the bottom of the interface, a supervisor overseeing a team of technicians can easily select a single route (in this case, route 36). The map server then redraws the map with only that route displayed and changes the extent to cover just the geographic area of the single route.

The route is drawn in a color that contrasts with the streets, and the stops are shown as numbered dots that correspond to the locations where the technician will be working. Zooming in to one route turns on street labels.

Once the map in the Web browser window is zoomed in close enough to make individual stops discernible, the supervisor can select the Identify tool and get more information from the route database directly through the browser.

Supervisors and managers at the headquarters in Los Angeles can easily see where each technician is supposed to be going on any given day.

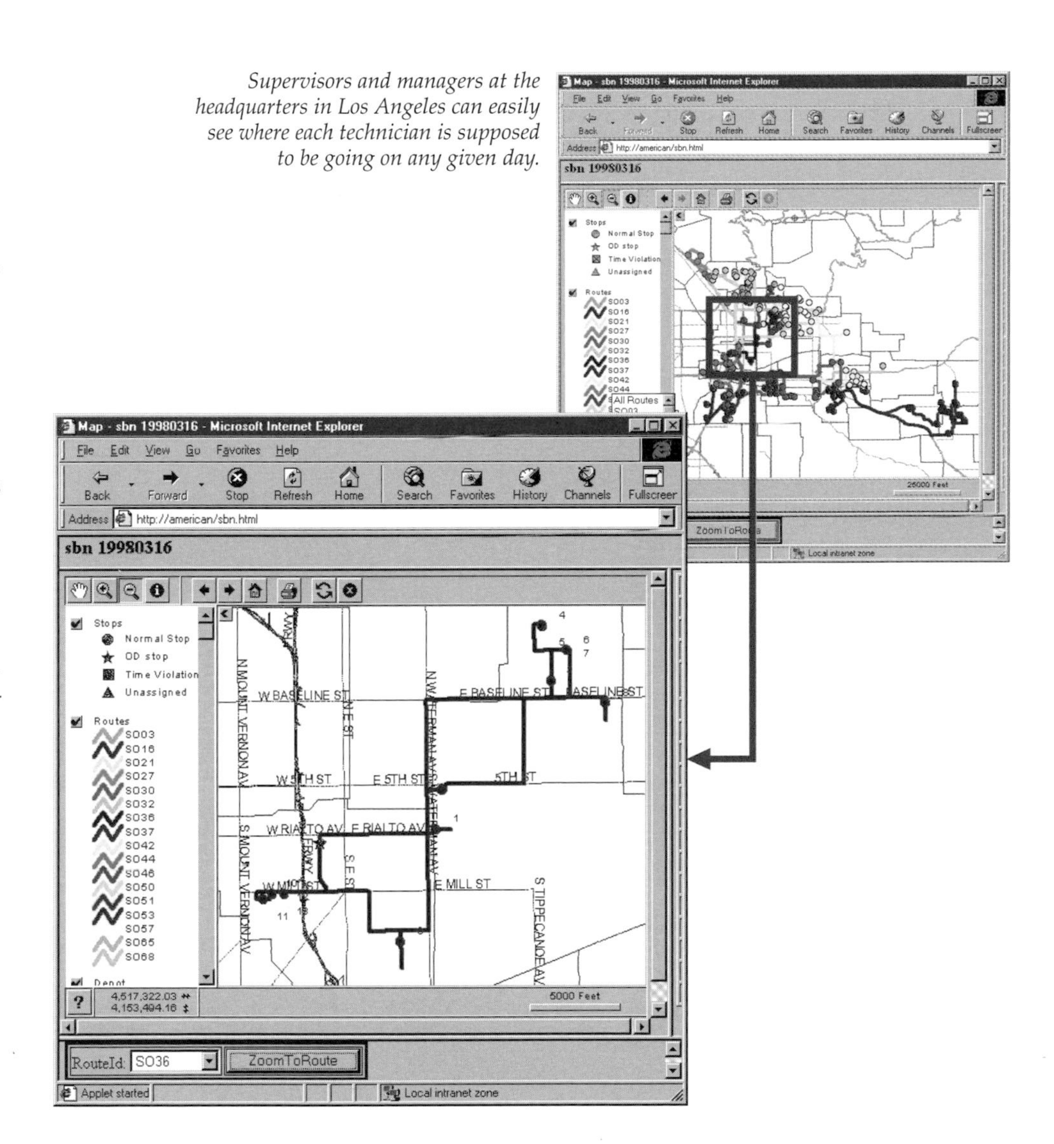

Identifying routes and stops

The Identify tool is one of the most useful features of the interface. Supervisors need only point and click on a route or a stop to bring up its associated information. This is significant because it means they can access all the information they need through the Web browser, instead of having to run separate routines on various software packages.

Presented in a table in the Web browser to the right of the map, this information includes a number of details about the routes and stops. For example, the route table seen in the lower graphic tells the supervisor, among other things, that the route is about 17 miles long, has eighteen stops, and should take the technician 393 minutes (about six and a half hours) to complete.

Clicking the Identify tool on a stop tells the supervisor its address, its distance from the previous stop, and the type of work to be performed there.

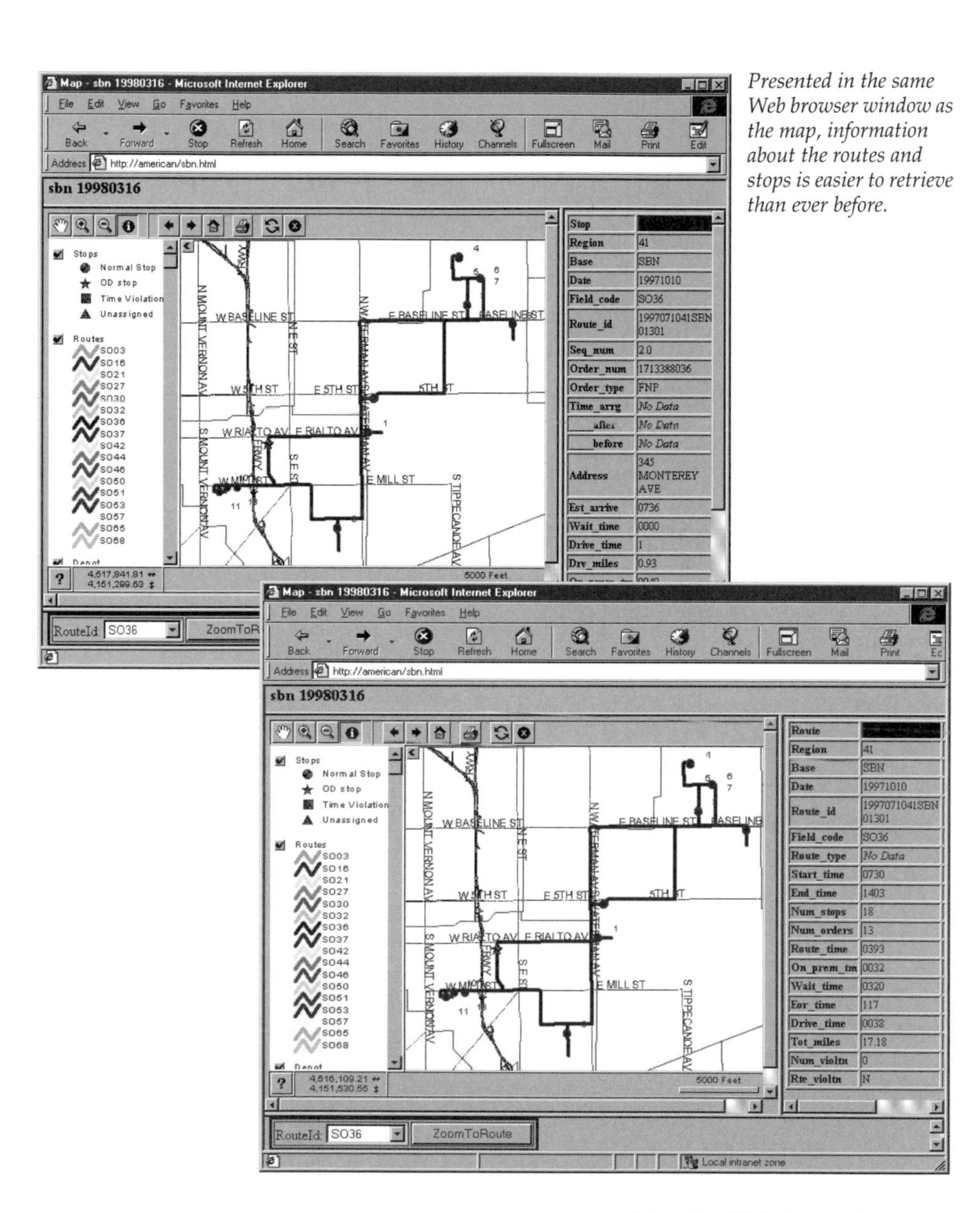

Presented in the same Web browser window as the map, information about the routes and stops is easier to retrieve than ever before.

Map output

In the future, route maps may be automatically printed and provided to the technicians.

Since the routes for a particular region differ considerably from day to day, as the maps at the right show, automation of the process has made everyone's lives much easier.

Feedback from the trenches

To date, there is generally good acceptance of the GRID system by the region supervisors and field service technicians. SoCalGas feels that the GRID system will provide the following benefits: the ability to schedule more service orders per day, and the ability to improve customer satisfaction by meeting service order time arrangements.

And in addition to the improvements in customer service, management will have access through the intranet to a useful tool for planning and monitoring field service operations.

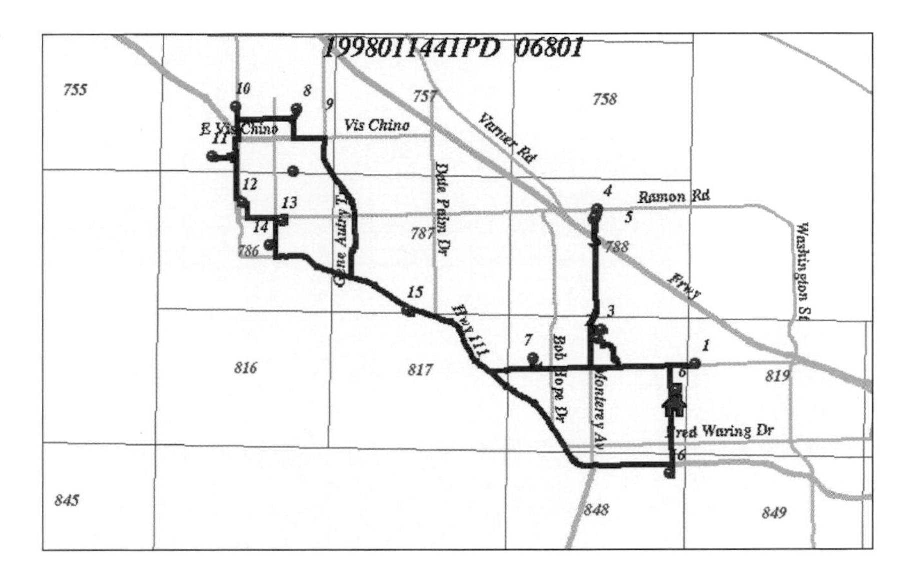

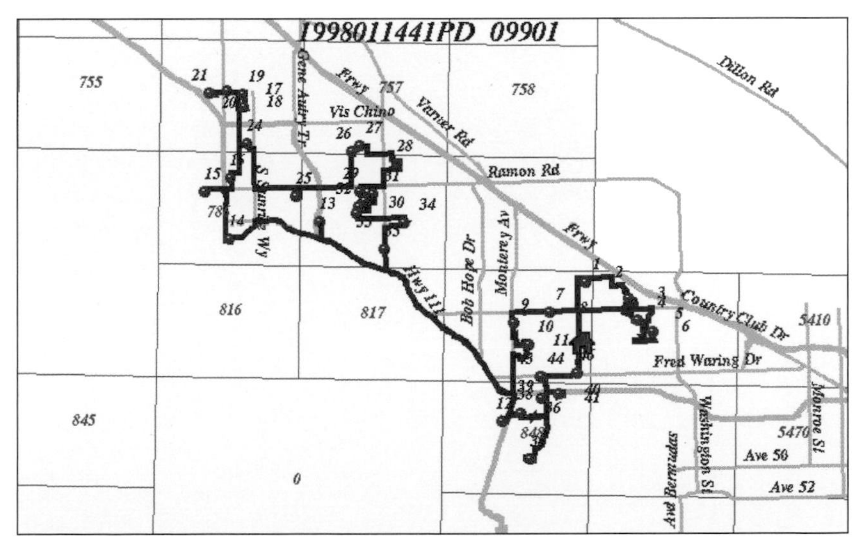

These two maps show the difference in routes that a day makes. Given two different sets of stops, the automated routing system returns two route paths that differ significantly.

Acknowledgments

Thanks to Gil Muramatsu and Julie Wunderlich of Southern California Gas Company, and to Jim McKinny and Ming Zhao of ESRI.

Southern California Gas Company's Web site is at www.socalgas.com.

Chapter 12

Power struggle

Electric utilities are at their most vulnerable during tropical storms, tornadoes, and hurricanes. In the immediate aftermath of a destructive storm, when panic and chaos are the norm, utilities must react quickly to the situation, whatever challenges it presents. At such moments, they need accurate information and they need it immediately.

In this chapter, you'll see how a pioneering power utility in hurricane country developed an intranet client to its GIS database that they used when a hurricane wiped out a power station.

Alabama Power

Southern Company is America's largest electric utility concern. Its six affiliates provide electricity to customers in Alabama, Florida, Georgia, and Mississippi.

One of those affiliates, Alabama Power Company, was among the first utilities in the world to use GIS for asset and facilities management across the enterprise—in real estate operations, transmission, distribution, and marketing.

By 1997, the old Alabama Power GIS team (renamed Southern GIS) had amassed gigabytes of spatial data, but few employees could access it. Using off-the-shelf GIS software and the Internet, Southern GIS solved the problem.

Although relatively rare, storms like the 1998 Hurricane Georges can do damage that lasts decades.

Spanning the enterprise

The Southern GIS team added a special server extension to its massive GIS database, making it accessible to all computer-equipped Southern Company employees through a standard Web browser.

The database was published on the company's secure intranet in the form of maps that could be queried and manipulated by anyone within the company.

The database included all of the layers that could be used by both casual and hard-core users.

The system also allowed Southern GIS to publish more maps focused on specific tasks, such as the response to Hurricane Georges, where information has to be disseminated as soon as it comes in.

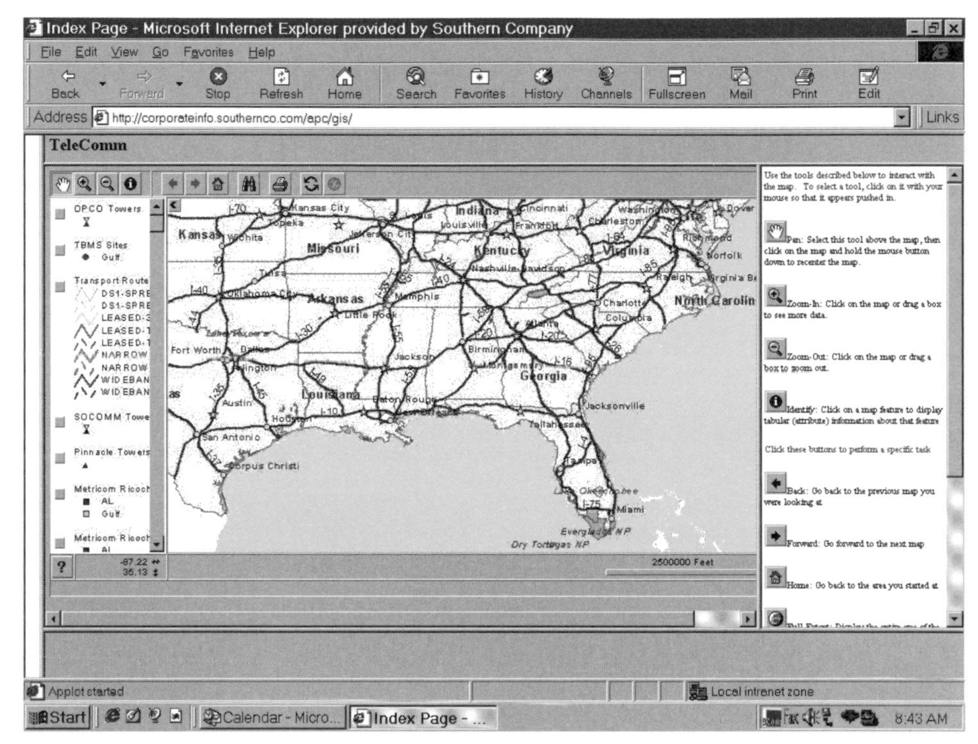

This is the default map view that a user sees after logging onto the Southern GIS map server. The extent covers the entire Southern Company service area and gives the beginning user a guide to the tools available.

Anticipating the inevitable

About once or twice a year along the Gulf Coast of the United States, a particularly strong hurricane will aim itself directly at places like Dauphin Island, Alabama, where Southern Company has a distribution substation serving the residents of the island.

When Hurricane Georges, a category 2 storm, struck Dauphin Island, it was estimated that the storm surge would push several hundred yards onto the shore, flooding the island and possibly destroying the electric facilities that serve some seven hundred homes in the area. (Based on data provided by the National Oceanic and Atmospheric Administration and the Alabama Coastal Services Center, such severe flooding would only be expected every hundred years.) Southern GIS used data on previous hurricanes to substantiate the estimate and provided information for planning service restoration.

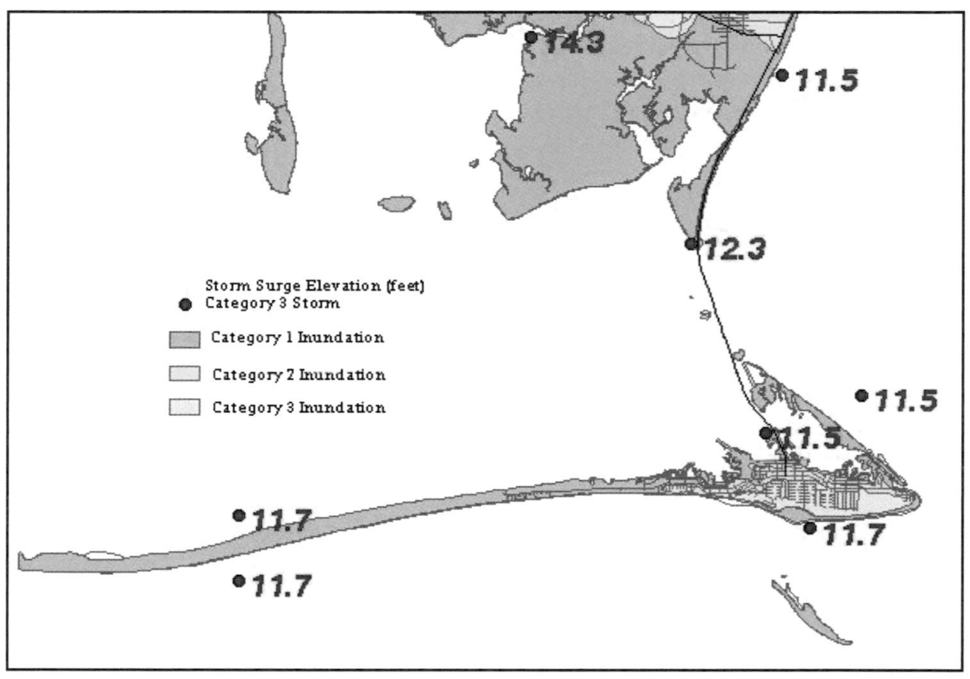

Dauphin Island, Alabama, is about as exposed to a hurricane as a piece of land can be. Ninety percent of the island is covered with water once every hundred years by storm surge. The entire island is expected to be submerged every five hundred years.

Going mobile near Mobile

When the call came from Mobile Division to Alabama Power headquarters in Birmingham, the news was bad. Hurricane Georges had hit all 53 miles of Alabama's short coastline, and hit them hard. The company's facilities on Dauphin Island—a sliver of land that forms the outer banks of Mobile Bay—had been weakened by the gale-force winds, then swept away by the storm surge. An immediate and massive response would be required to get electric service back up and running.

Staging areas were needed for the efforts, which would take several days and could only begin when the weather had subsided. As the hurricane raged on, managers in Mobile were busy pulling up various maps from the GIS database, determining the best locations for these staging areas. It was from these locations that work crews and materials would be dispatched to restore service to Southern Company customers.

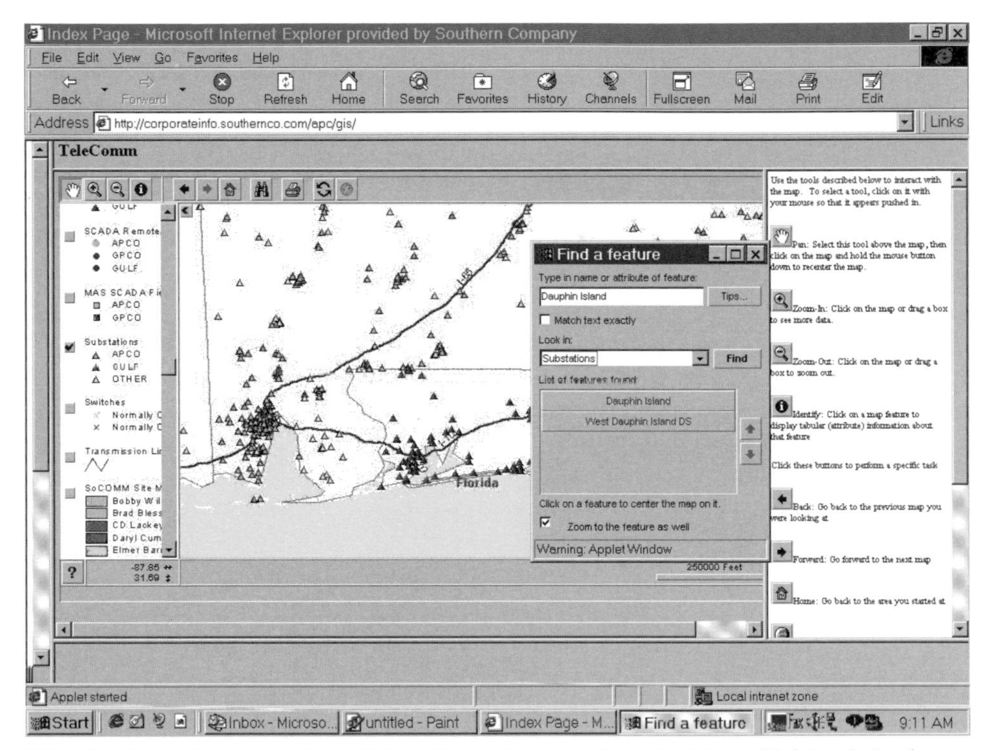

When Hurricane Georges wiped out Alabama Power Company electric facilities and left hundreds of households in the dark, the company's GIS database helped managers mobilize a sizeable workforce.

Keeping the crews fed and housed

Once the coordinators in Mobile had established the staging areas, they began identifying restaurants and hotels in the area that had not been damaged by the hurricane and to which electric service could be restored quickly. From these lists, they arranged accommodations for the several hundred technicians and emergency response experts already converging on the scene.

Even crews brought in from other Southern Company affiliates in nearby states used the system to print maps giving directions to the scene.

So, as they've been doing for the past seven years, Southern GIS proved how valuable the right information at the right time can be in emergency situations, and how dispersing information over a large corporation can save time and money and improve customer service.

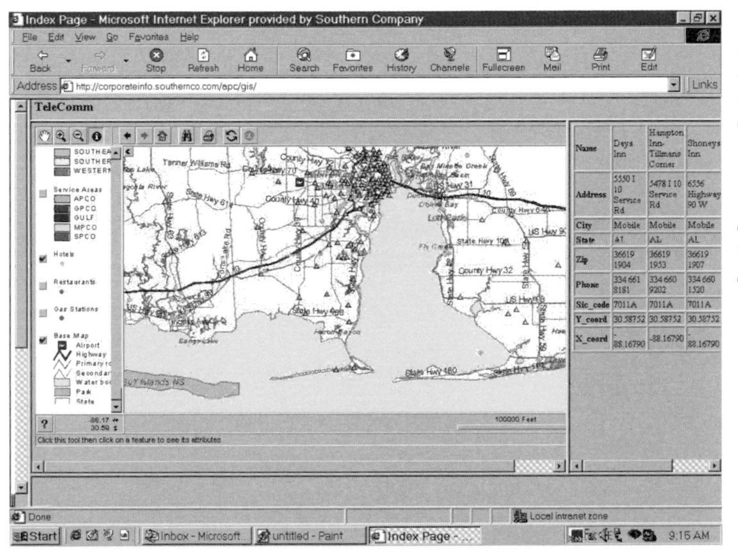

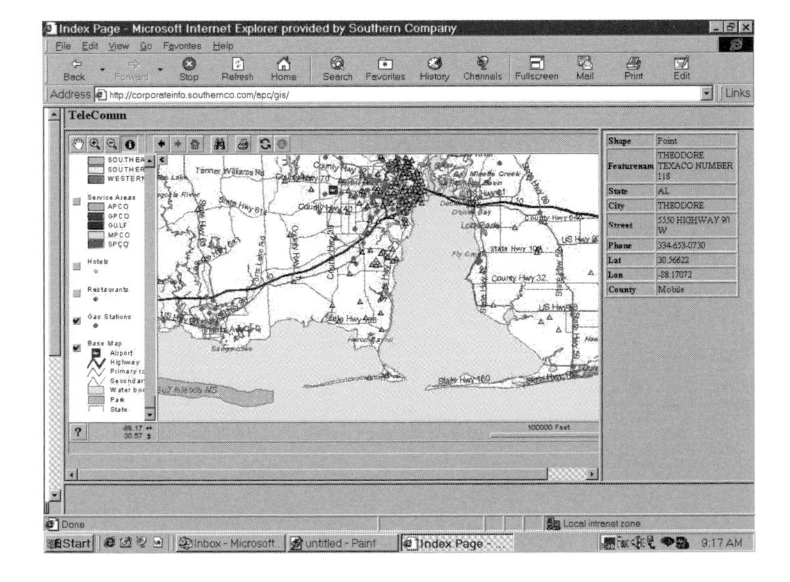

Querying a database located more than 250 miles away in Birmingham, Alabama, emergency response managers in Mobile used this Web-based tool to locate staging areas and accommodations for work crews coming from all over the Southeast.

Conclusion

The benefits of GIS are known to be enormous. In the situation described, it's difficult to quantify the actual benefit in dollars, but it can be estimated.

For starters, the lost revenue for a thousand average residential customers is about three to four thousand dollars per day. However, when commercial and industrial customers are included in the equation, the total economic loss is much higher.

In addition to the cost of losing customer loyalty, a crew with heavy equipment costs the company thousands of dollars a day. If the routing increases efficiency by just one day, savings can approach $100,000.

Hardware

At the time of writing, the application was running on a dual Pentium 300-MHz Web server with 256 megabytes of RAM. The total amount of spatial data available to users exceeds 16.7 gigabytes. As the demands on the system increase, there are plans to increase the capacity of the system by adding servers.

Software

ArcView GIS version 3.1

ArcExplorer™ version 1.1

ArcView IMS components

MapObjects IMS version 2.0 components

Microsoft IIS 4

Microsoft FrontPage®

Acknowledgments

Thanks to Karen McDonald and Vincent Petix of Southern GIS.

Chapter 13

Electrifying Sweden

High-voltage transmission lines are the volume transporters of the utility industry. These lines, each carrying from 200,000 to 400,000 volts, move electricity from generating plants to local distribution centers. Here, the power is reduced to voltages that can be used in homes and businesses to power electric lights, heat or cool homes, and run appliances.

In this chapter, you'll see how a system developed by a state-owned Scandinavian power company is used to help deliver electricity safely and inexpensively to its citizens and sometimes even to neighboring countries.

Power to the Swedes

Svenska Kraftnät, owned and operated by the Swedish government, was launched in 1992 to manage the nation's electric transmission network, as well as the links to the transmission networks of neighboring countries.

The company is charged with purchasing electricity from power-generating facilities, and then delivering the power to several hundred distribution companies—in effect, franchise customers of Svenska Kraftnät.

It also maintains the connections to the power grids of neighboring Norway, Denmark, and Finland, so that power may be bought or sold between Scandinavian nations whenever the need arises.

The power lines of Svenska Kraftnät deliver power to all of Sweden and connect to the power grids of other Nordic countries.

The Swedish electricity market

Svenska Kraftnät faces unique information management challenges. For starters, the company is required by law to purchase power from each of the more than three hundred power-generating firms in Sweden (many of them quite small) according to a strict set of pricing guidelines.

The national high-voltage grid connects to Norway, Finland, Denmark, and Germany. So the information system used to manage this part of the grid must take into account these countries' concerns, policies, and laws having to do with international power swapping.

Svenska Kraftnät is also responsible for building new transmission facilities. In a nation as socially conscious as Sweden, this means ensuring that high-voltage lines do not pass too closely to concentrations of women and children.

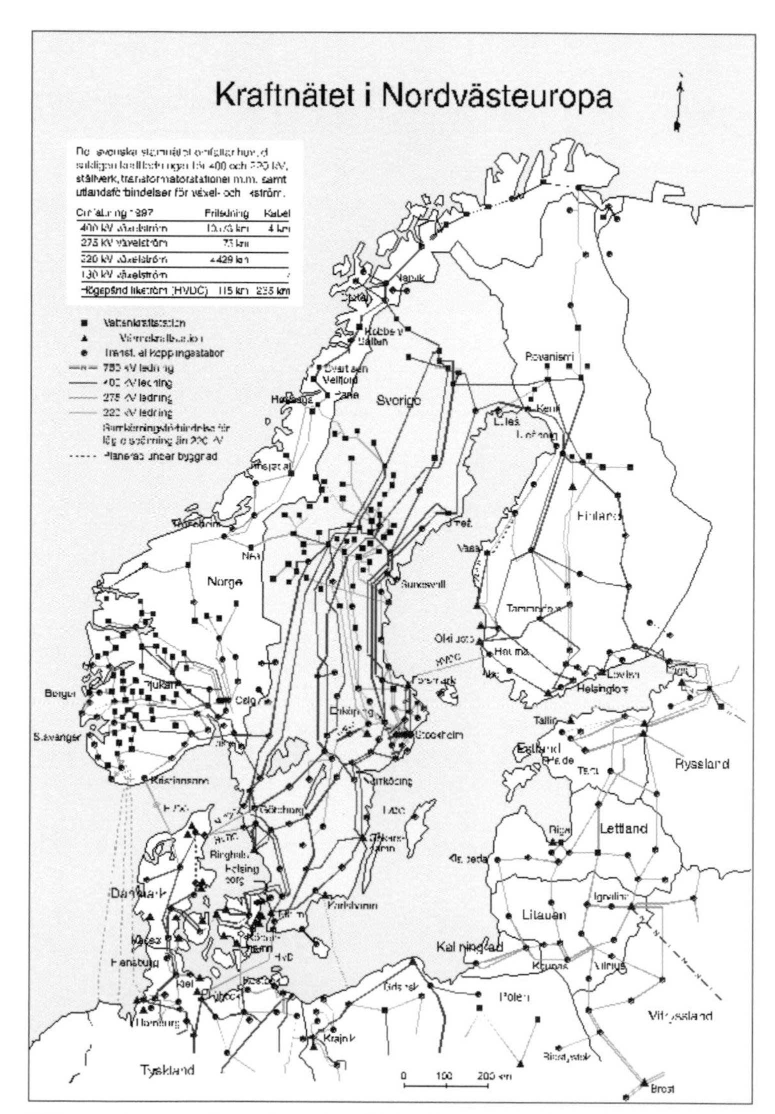

This overview map shows the various high-voltage transmission lines of Sweden and neighboring countries.

Introducing GISELA

Using base map data from many national GIS data providers, and software from both ESRI and ESRI–Sweden, Svenska Kraftnät developed an application called GISELA for managing all aspects of the national high-voltage transmission system.

Unlike the United States, where GIS users have had access to digital land base geography for some time at nominal cost, the geography of Sweden has only recently been completely digitized. Because Svenska Kraftnät is affiliated with the government, it was given access to data developed for military purposes (GeoPres) by the Swedish military. As a result, the GISELA project has emerged as one of the first major nonmilitary applications of GeoPres on a national level in Sweden.

From the GISELA client, users throughout the organization can access information about any aspect of the transmission system through an easy-to-use map-based interface.

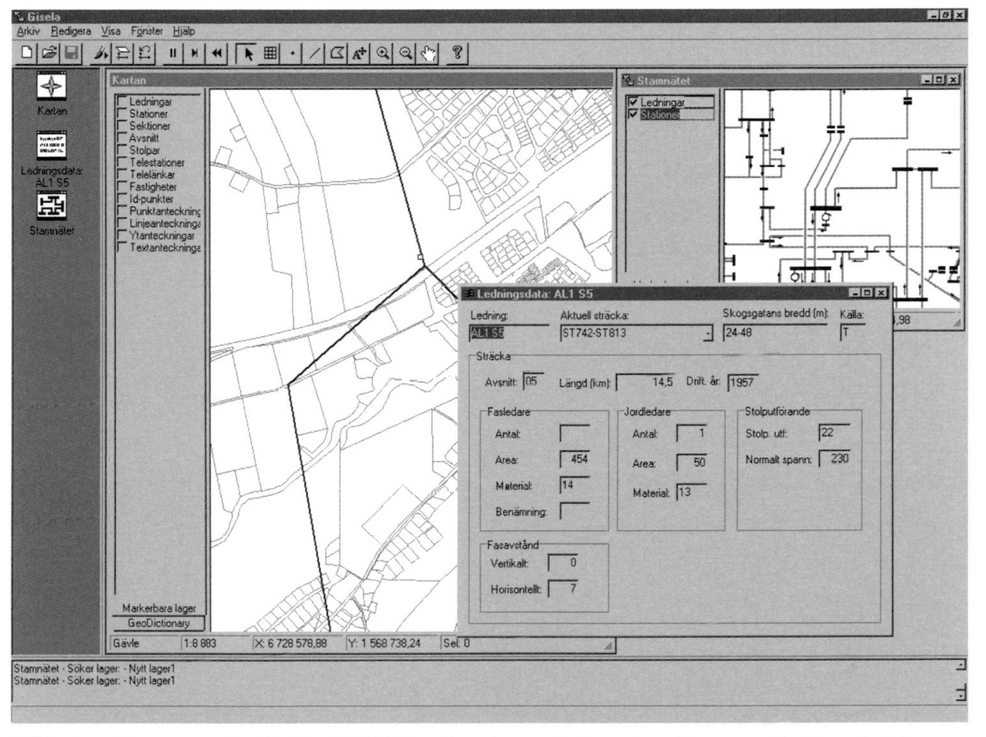

All information concerning the Swedish high-voltage transmission network is accessible through this interface. Here, information about a segment of wire is seen by clicking on the segment as it appears superimposed on a parcel map.

Linking spatial and schematic views

Before GIS, Svenska Kraftnät relied on schematic drawings (stored as CAD files) to manage its facilities. While these schematic views did represent the equipment, they were not linked to geography and so did not show the various parts at a correct scale in relation to other parts.

With GISELA, Svenska Kraftnät still has access to the schematic drawings needed by the engineering team. But now they also have the same data linked to geography, so that features can be displayed in either straight schematic or geographic views. The data only has to be updated in a single spatial database.

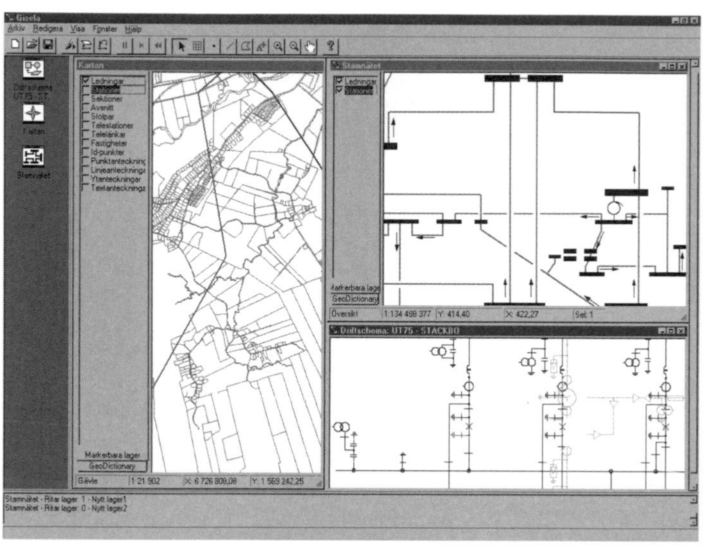

By clicking on a transmission line on the map at the left, the user can see the same segment displayed on two different schematic (nongeographic) diagrams.

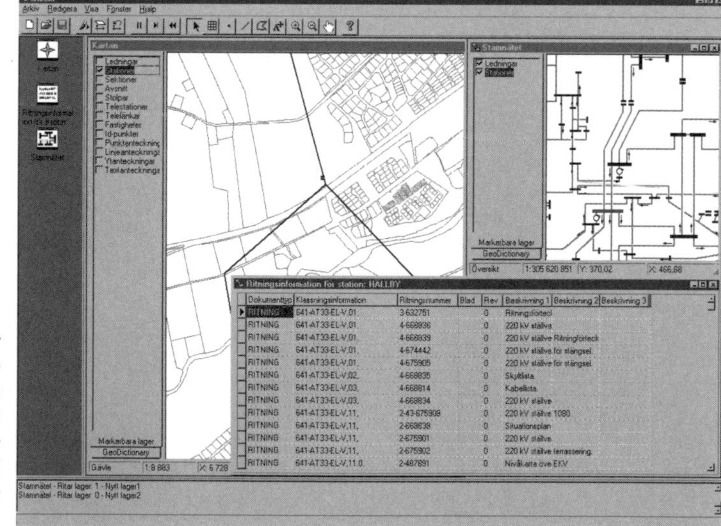

GISELA allows a user to click on an object to find all CAD drawings attached to it. The CAD drawings can then be viewed on-screen and components can be identified.

Lines across the land

Most of the land its lines must cross are not owned by Svenska Kraftnät, so GISELA also stores information about property ownership.

All real estate crossed by the power lines of Svenska Kraftnät can be identified automatically by defining a buffer zone width around the lines. Property owners can be notified when Svenska Kraftnät has to send a crew onto the property to perform maintenance or repairs.

The database also includes sociodemographic information, so this same functionality can be used to calculate things like the number of women and children within reach of electromagnetic radiation.

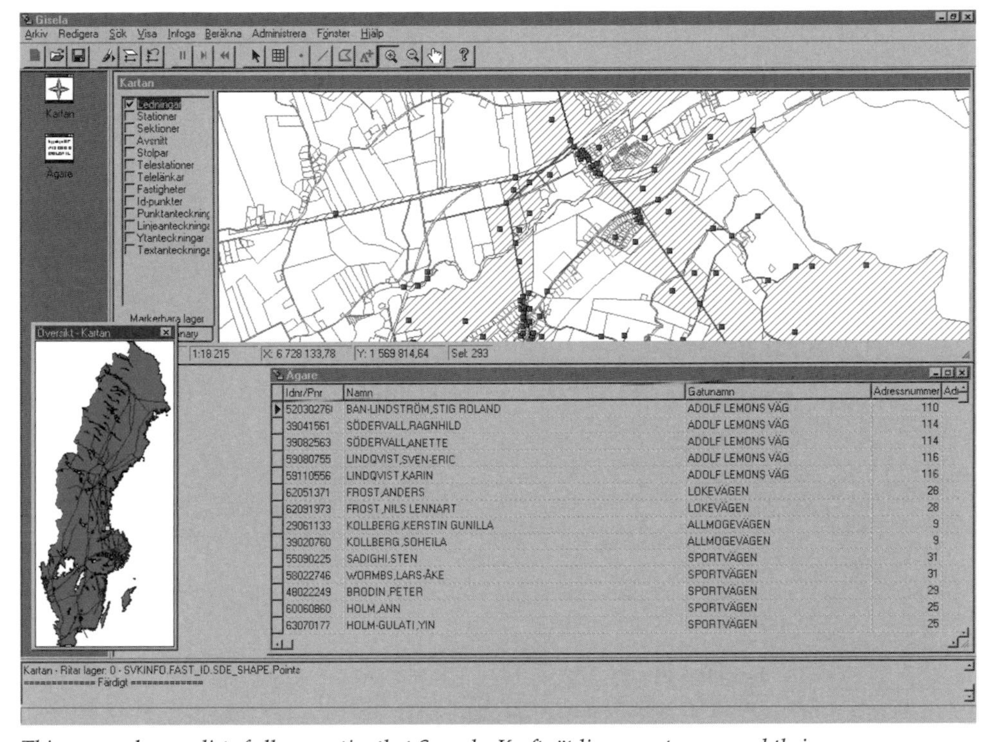

This screen shows a list of all properties that Svenska Kraftnät lines must cross, and their owners.

Hardware

Server

Windows NT clients

Software

MapObjects

Spatial Database Engine

GeoPres™

SOLE

Acknowledgments

Thanks to Lars Skog of ESRI–Sweden and to Anders Åslund of LandFocus IS.

Introducing ArcFM

ARC/INFO databases have been the de facto standard in the energy distribution field for many years. Their effective application required extensive customization to make them easily usable and productive within the utility environment. With the release of ArcFM software from ESRI, utilities now have an "out-of-the-box" solution that allows them to get a useful GIS up and running in a fraction of the time previously required. ArcFM—for Arc Facilities Manager—is an ARC/INFO-based software application designed specifically to meet the unique data management needs of the utility industry.

From AM/FM to ArcFM

Gas and electric utilities require sophisticated systems capable of modeling and analyzing energy distribution and transmission networks. Beginning in the early 1980s, utilities began using computerized geographic information systems like ARC/INFO for this purpose. These early GIS applications, called AM/FM for automated mapping/facilities management, ran only on high-performance computers, were written in difficult procedural programming languages, and stored geographic features in flat files and attributes in relational databases.

With the advent of powerful desktop computers and easier-to-use, object-oriented programming languages, AM/FM systems gradually migrated to the client/server model, which allowed utilities to distribute GIS functionality to a much wider user base. But some limitations remained. Geographic features were still required to be stored separately from their attributes, and the programming languages were not easy to customize using standard methods.

ArcFM brings together several important technologies to deliver the first truly open and extensible client/server GIS solution for utilities.

Changes in GIS software technology

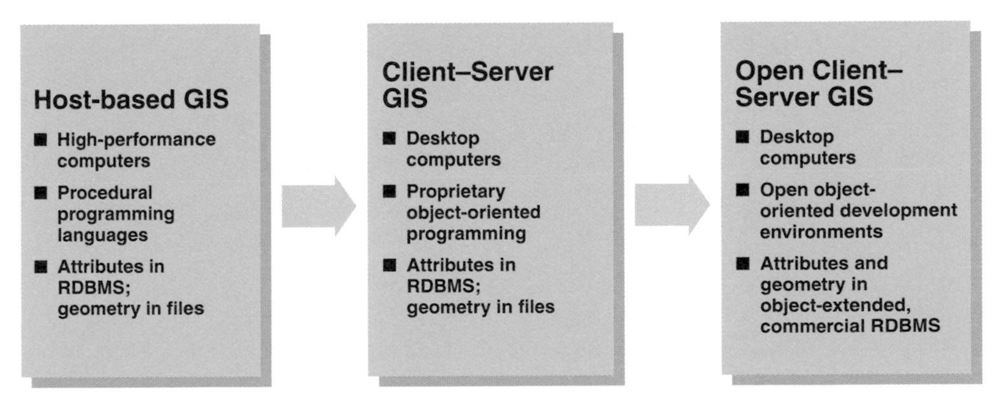

How ArcFM works

In ArcFM, all of a utility's data—both spatial and attribute—can be stored in a single relational database management system (RDBMS). This is possible because of ESRI's Spatial Database Engine (SDE), a technology that enables spatial data to be stored, managed, and retrieved quickly from such leading commercial database management systems as Oracle, Microsoft SQL Server, Sybase, IBM DB2®, and Informix®.

ArcFM also uses the RuleBase Engine (RBE), a system for encoding the specific business rules of a utility organization. ArcFM comes with ready-to-use rule sets for electric and gas utilities, as well as water and wastewater, for constructing a database quickly and accurately. For example, the RBE for gas utilities would prevent the person building the GIS database from connecting a 4-inch pipe to a 1-inch pipe without the proper reducer. This simple concept represents a major breakthrough in data control and consistency across the organization.

The ArcFM application itself is noteworthy because it is built using Microsoft Visual Basic, one of the most widely used (and easily learned) programming languages. This means it can be easily modified by utility programmers without additional training, and it easily integrates with other business applications already in place.

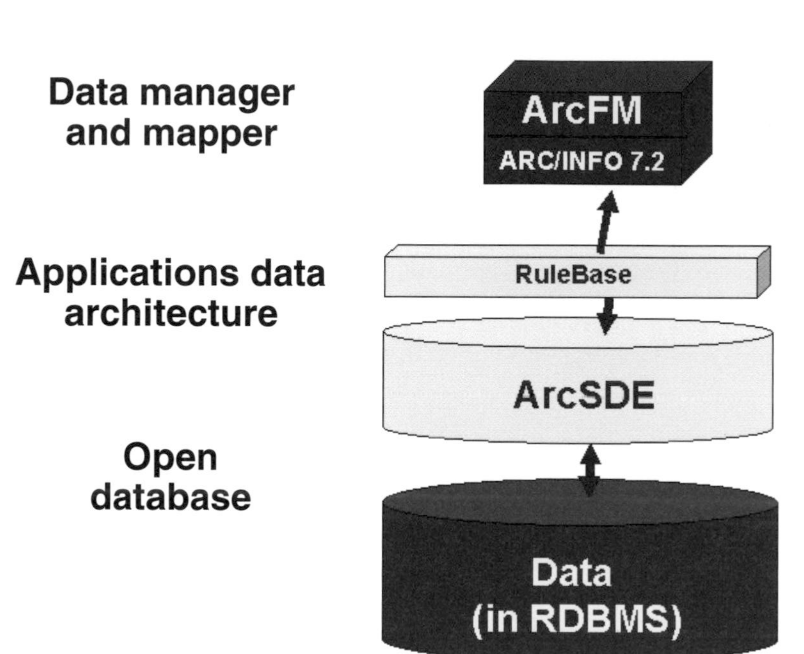

How ArcFM is used

Integrating maps and spatial data into the workflow utility organization, spatial data becomes part of the entire work process. ArcFM provides all the capabilities required to achieve this integration. From its menu-driven user interface, employees across all departments have access to a set of tools for creating and updating databases, querying the data based on known attributes, performing standard analyses, and producing accurate and readable maps.

Editing and adding features

A utility GIS database is not a static thing; even after its initial development, new features must be added continually. ArcFM speeds up this process.

A number of tools simplify the process of adding or moving geographic features in the GIS database. And the RuleBase Engine prevents the user from adding or editing anything in a way that violates the standard way of doing things, thus maintaining the integrity of the database.

Updating attributes

In ArcFM, the Attribute Update tool allows the user to make changes to the attribute database by clicking on the feature on the map. For example, if a transformer is damaged in a lightning storm and must be replaced, the user can simply click on the transformer on the map with the attribute update tool and enter details about the new piece of equipment.

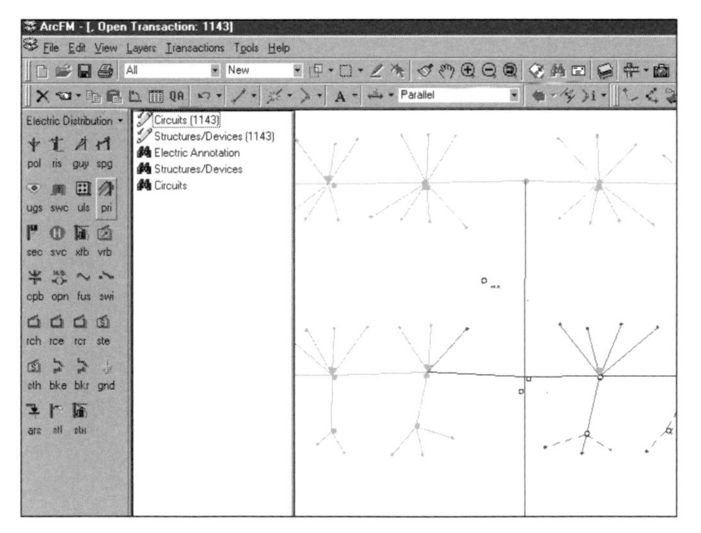

Editing

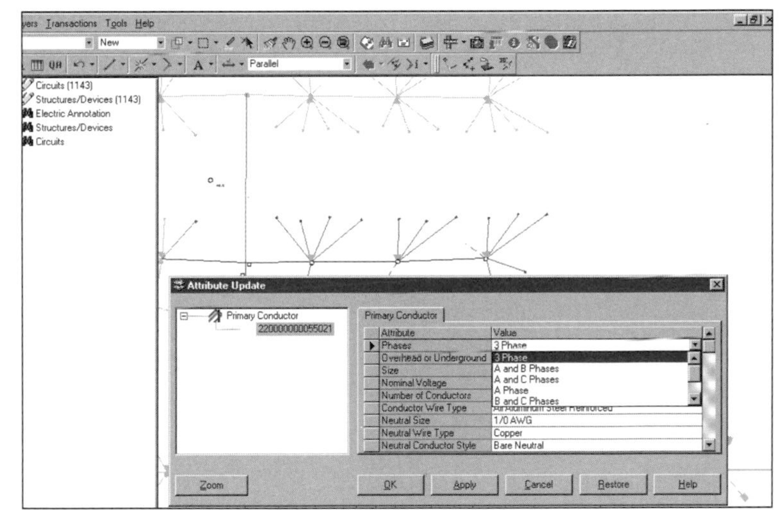

Updating

The Query Builder

The ArcFM Query Builder is a useful tool for locating features by attributes. The tool is enabled when there is an open map document and a layer in that document has been selected. The Query Builder could be used to answer questions like "How many valves are due for inspection on the west side of town?"

The Trace Tool

The Trace Tool is used to determine which features are connected in an electric or gas network. The tool identifies different types of upstream and downstream devices (such as customers, protective devices, stopping points, and valves) from a chosen starting point. This tool can aid in validating connectivity to ensure that the GIS database is topologically connected.

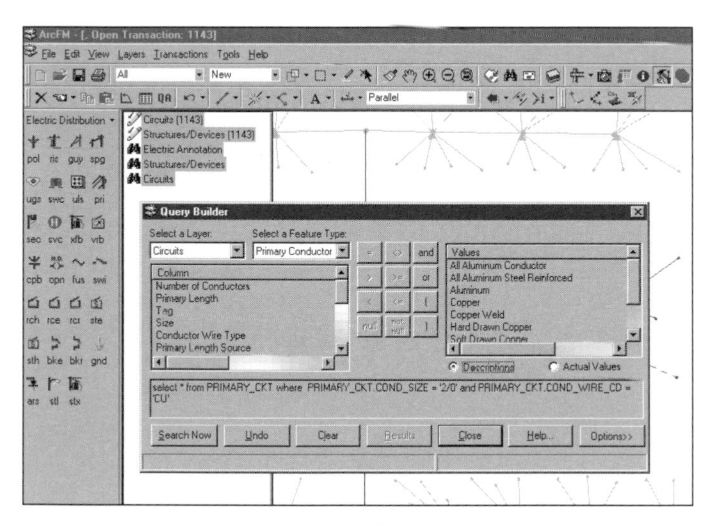

Querying

Tracing

Versioning

When many people around the organization all have editing capability on a database, as is the case in a typical ArcFM scenario, discrepancies or conflicts can arise if two users are both editing the same feature at the same time. ArcFM software keeps track of any conflicts and provides a form for resolving the conflict. It does this by keeping track of the different "versions" of edits and presenting users with a form for selecting the correct version to use.

For more information about the capabilities and future product direction of ArcFM, please refer to www.esri.com/software/arcfm.

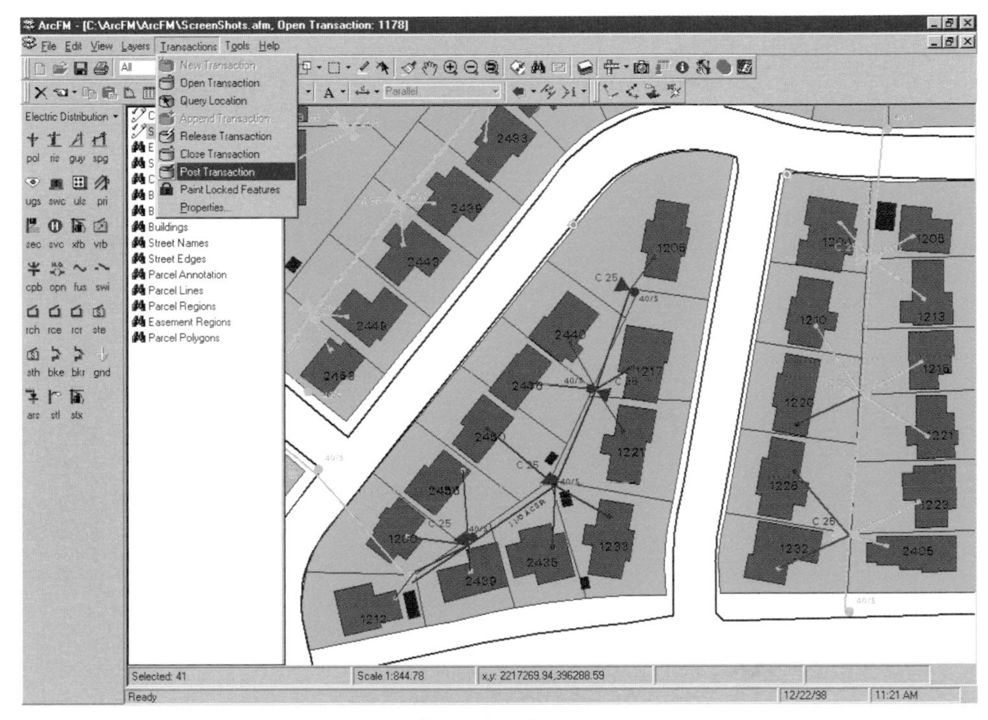

Versioning